TO HEAR HIS VOICE: A MASS JOURNAL FOR CATHOLIC KIDS

YEAR C, PART TWO (SOLEMNITY OF THE HOLY TRINITY THROUGH CHRIST THE KING)

GINNY KOCHIS

CONTENTS

INTRODUCTION

Mass isn't easy.

It's long. The pews are hard. Your mind keeps wandering back to Minecraft, or your favorite animal, or that book you stayed up reading last night. Going to Mass might be the last thing on your list of priorities. But truthfully?

It's one of the best moments of your life.

Our Catholic faith is a blessing. Through the Church, God gives us the fullness of the Truth. He gives us grace through the Sacraments and the sacrifice of the Mass.

The Mass is a beautiful gift God gives us. This journal will help you open it up.

It would be easier for the world to survive without the sun than to do without Holy Mass. - St. Pio of Petroclina (Padre Pio)

A Note to Parents (And Kids)

To Hear His Voice is designed to fit your family's needs. This newly revised second edition does not include calendar dates listed for the Sundays and Holy Days of Obligation. Rather, chapters are titled according to the day's position in the liturgical year. For instance, this edition for the second half of Year C begins with the Solemnity of the Most Holy Trinity and ends with The Solemnity of Our Lord Jesus Christ, King of the Universe.

Chapters contain:

- each Sunday's readings
- space to draw, journal, or take notes
- discussion questions to help you delve into the meaning of the Scriptures
- writing prompts to help you and your family apply Church teaching
- prayers and suggestions for evangelization

Your children can use this book however they like

- before Mass to prepare
- during Mass to follow along
- after Mass to recap and review

Feel free to have your children write, draw, or dictate their thoughts and answers. How your family uses this journal is completely up to you.

THE SOLEMNITY OF THE MOST HOLY TRINITY

A **Reading from the Book of Proverbs**
    Prv 8:22-31

Thus says the wisdom of God:
"The LORD possessed me, the beginning of his ways,
the forerunner of his prodigies of long ago;
from of old I was poured forth,
at the first, before the earth.
When there were no depths I was brought forth,
when there were no fountains or springs of water;
before the mountains were settled into place,
before the hills, I was brought forth;
while as yet the earth and fields were not made,
nor the first clods of the world.

"When the Lord established the heavens I was there,
when he marked out the vault over the face of the deep;
when he made firm the skies above,
when he fixed fast the foundations of the earth;
when he set for the sea its limit,
so that the waters should not transgress his command;
then was I beside him as his craftsman,
and I was his delight day by day,

playing before him all the while,
playing on the surface of his earth;
and I found delight in the human race."

WHEN A WRITER GIVES human characteristics to a non-human object or idea, it is called personification. What is personified in this passage? What human traits does it have?

Responsorial Psalm

Ps 8:4-5, 6-7, 8-9

R (2a) O Lord, our God, how wonderful your name in all the earth!
When I behold your heavens, the work of your fingers,
the moon and the stars which you set in place —
What is man that you should be mindful of him,
or the son of man that you should care for him?
R O Lord, our God, how wonderful your name in all the earth!
You have made him little less than the angels,
and crowned him with glory and honor.
You have given him rule over the works of your hands,
putting all things under his feet:
R O Lord, our God, how wonderful your name in all the earth!
All sheep and oxen,
yes, and the beasts of the field,
The birds of the air, the fishes of the sea,
and whatever swims the paths of the seas.
R O Lord, our God, how wonderful your name in all the earth!

IN TODAY'S PSALM, the psalmist lists all of the ways in which he encounters God's glory. What about you? Where have you experienced, seen, or felt the glory of God?

A reading from the Letter of St. Paul to the Romans

Rom 5:1-5

Brothers and sisters:
Therefore, since we have been justified by faith,
we have peace with God through our Lord Jesus Christ,
through whom we have gained access by faith
to this grace in which we stand,
and we boast in hope of the glory of God.
Not only that, but we even boast of our afflictions,
knowing that affliction produces endurance,
and endurance, proven character,
and proven character, hope,
and hope does not disappoint,
because the love of God has been poured out into our hearts
through the Holy Spirit that has been given to us.

DEFINE THE WORD "AFFLICTION." According to St. Paul, how are they beneficial to us and our growth in faith?

A reading from the holy Gospel according to John

Jn 16:12-15

Jesus said to his disciples:
"I have much more to tell you, but you cannot bear it now.
But when he comes, the Spirit of truth,
he will guide you to all truth.
He will not speak on his own,
but he will speak what he hears,
and will declare to you the things that are coming.
He will glorify me,
because he will take from what is mine and declare it to you.
Everything that the Father has is mine;
for this reason I told you that he will take from what is mine
and declare it to you."

WHY DOES Jesus send the Holy Spirit to the apostles? Provide a specific example from the text.

Pray:

Heavenly Father, thank you for the gift of the Holy Spirit. Thank you for wisdom and perseverance, which come from the Holy Spirit. Grant that I may always be open to you and to the words you speak in my heart. Amen.

Think:

What connection can you find between the afflictions St. Paul writes about in the first reading and Jesus' words to the apostles in the Gospel? For help, review your definition of the word affliction.

Go Forth:

Before bed this week, spend five minutes recalling your day. Look for the moments in which you saw God's glory. Record them here.

THE DEVIL IS
AFRAID OF US
WHEN WE
PRAY AND MAKE SACRIFICES.

-St. Anthony of Padua

2

THE SOLEMNITY OF THE MOST HOLY BODY AND BLOOD OF CHRIST

 reading from the Book of Genesis
Gn 14:18-20

In those days, Melchizedek, king of Salem, brought out bread and wine,
and being a priest of God Most High,
he blessed Abram with these words:
"Blessed be Abram by God Most High,
the creator of heaven and earth;
and blessed be God Most High,
who delivered your foes into your hand."
Then Abram gave him a tenth of everything.

WHAT SACRAMENTS ARE PRE-FIGURED HERE? In other words, which sacraments do you see reflected in Abram's meeting with Melchizedek? For an extra challenge, consider: why is this foreshadowing important?

Responsorial Psalm

Ps 110:1, 2, 3, 4

R (4b) You are a priest forever, in the line of Melchizedek.
The LORD said to my Lord: "Sit at my right hand
till I make your enemies your footstool."
R You are a priest forever, in the line of Melchizedek.
The scepter of your power the LORD will stretch forth from Zion:
"Rule in the midst of your enemies."
R You are a priest forever, in the line of Melchizedek.
"Yours is princely power in the day of your birth, in holy splendor;
before the daystar, like the dew, I have begotten you."
R You are a priest forever, in the line of Melchizedek.
The LORD has sworn, and he will not repent:
"You are a priest forever, according to the order of Melchizedek."
R You are a priest forever, in the line of Melchizedek.

With your parents' permission, research Apostolic Succession. What is the connection between today's Psalm and Apostolic Succession?

A reading from the first Letter of St. Paul to the Corinthians

I Cor 11:23-26

Brothers and sisters:
I received from the Lord what I also handed on to you,
that the Lord Jesus, on the night he was handed over,
took bread, and, after he had given thanks,
broke it and said, "This is my body that is for you.
Do this in remembrance of me."
In the same way also the cup, after supper, saying,
"This cup is the new covenant in my blood.
Do this, as often as you drink it, in remembrance of me."
For as often as you eat this bread and drink the cup,
you proclaim the death of the Lord until he comes.

CONSIDERING St. Paul wrote this Letter sometime around the year 53 AD, what conclusion can you come to about the language used in the Liturgy of the Eucharist?

Sequence

Lauda Sion

Laud, O Zion, your salvation,
Laud with hymns of exultation,
Christ, your king and shepherd true:

Bring him all the praise you know,
He is more than you bestow.
Never can you reach his due.

Special theme for glad thanksgiving
Is the quick'ning and the living
Bread today before you set:

From his hands of old partaken,
As we know, by faith unshaken,
Where the Twelve at supper met.

Full and clear ring out your chanting,
Joy nor sweetest grace be wanting,
From your heart let praises burst:

For today the feast is holden,
When the institution olden
Of that supper was rehearsed.

Here the new law's new oblation,
By the new king's revelation,
Ends the form of ancient rite:

Now the new the old effaces,
Truth away the shadow chases,
Light dispels the gloom of night.

What he did at supper seated,
Christ ordained to be repeated,
His memorial ne'er to cease:

And his rule for guidance taking,
Bread and wine we hallow, making
Thus our sacrifice of peace.

This the truth each Christian learns,
Bread into his flesh he turns,
To his precious blood the wine:

Sight has fail'd, nor thought conceives,
But a dauntless faith believes,
Resting on a pow'r divine.

Here beneath these signs are hidden
Priceless things to sense forbidden;
Signs, not things are all we see:

Blood is poured and flesh is broken,
Yet in either wondrous token
Christ entire we know to be.

Whoso of this food partakes,
Does not rend the Lord nor breaks;
Christ is whole to all that taste:

Thousands are, as one, receivers,
One, as thousands of believers,
Eats of him who cannot waste.

Bad and good the feast are sharing,
Of what divers dooms preparing,
Endless death, or endless life.

Life to these, to those damnation,
See how like participation
Is with unlike issues rife.

When the sacrament is broken,
Doubt not, but believe 'tis spoken,
That each sever'd outward token
doth the very whole contain.

Nought the precious gift divides,
Breaking but the sign betides
Jesus still the same abides,
still unbroken does remain.

The shorter form of the sequence begins here.

Lo! the angel's food is given
To the pilgrim who has striven;
see the children's bread from heaven,
which on dogs may not be spent.

Truth the ancient types fulfilling,
Isaac bound, a victim willing,
Paschal lamb, its lifeblood spilling,
manna to the fathers sent.

Very bread, good shepherd, tend us,
Jesu, of your love befriend us,
You refresh us, you defend us,
Your eternal goodness send us
In the land of life to see.

You who all things can and know,
Who on earth such food bestow,
Grant us with your saints, though lowest,
Where the heav'nly feast you show,
Fellow heirs and guests to be. Amen. Alleluia.

A reading from the holy Gospel according to Luke

Lk 9:11b-17

Jesus spoke to the crowds about the kingdom of God,
and he healed those who needed to be cured.
As the day was drawing to a close,
the Twelve approached him and said,
"Dismiss the crowd
so that they can go to the surrounding villages and farms
and find lodging and provisions;
for we are in a deserted place here."
He said to them, "Give them some food yourselves."
They replied, "Five loaves and two fish are all we have,
unless we ourselves go and buy food for all these people."
Now the men there numbered about five thousand.
Then he said to his disciples,
"Have them sit down in groups of about fifty."

They did so and made them all sit down.
Then taking the five loaves and the two fish,
and looking up to heaven,
he said the blessing over them, broke them,
and gave them to the disciples to set before the crowd.
They all ate and were satisfied.
And when the leftover fragments were picked up,
they filled twelve wicker baskets.

IN WHAT WAY has God multiplied the blessings in your life?

Pray:

Lord, you have given us so many good gifts. Today, I want to thank you for the gift of Holy Mother Church and all you provide us through her. Grant, Lord, that I may always seek to be closer to you through the graces of the Sacraments and the sacrifice of the Mass. Amen.

Think:

With your parents' permission, research the concept of Typology in Scripture. How are today's readings an example of Biblical typology?

Go Forth:

Last week, you worked on recording the moments where you saw God's glory throughout the day. This week, focus on the blessings and miracles you see in your daily life. Write about them here.

THE MYSTERY
OF CHRIST
RUNS THE
RISK OF
BEING
MISBLEIVED
PRECISELY
BECAUSE IT IS
SO
WONDERFUL.
-St. Cyril of Alexandria

3

THIRTEENTH SUNDAY IN ORDINARY TIME

 reading from the first Book of Kings
1 Kgs 19:16b, 19-21

The LORD said to Elijah:
"You shall anoint Elisha, son of Shaphat of Abelmeholah,
as prophet to succeed you."

Elijah set out and came upon Elisha, son of Shaphat,
as he was plowing with twelve yoke of oxen;
he was following the twelfth.
Elijah went over to him and threw his cloak over him.
Elisha left the oxen, ran after Elijah, and said,
"Please, let me kiss my father and mother goodbye,
and I will follow you."
Elijah answered, "Go back!
Have I done anything to you?"
Elisha left him, and taking the yoke of oxen, slaughtered them;
he used the plowing equipment for fuel to boil their flesh,
and gave it to his people to eat.
Then Elisha left and followed Elijah as his attendant.

How is this exchange between Elijiah and Elisha an example of apostolic succession?

Responsorial Psalm

Ps 16:1-2, 5, 7-8, 9-10, 11

R (cf. 5a) You are my inheritance, O Lord.
Keep me, O God, for in you I take refuge;
I say to the LORD, "My Lord are you.
O LORD, my allotted portion and my cup,
you it is who hold fast my lot."
R You are my inheritance, O Lord.
I bless the LORD who counsels me;
even in the night my heart exhorts me.
I set the LORD ever before me;
with him at my right hand I shall not be disturbed.
R You are my inheritance, O Lord.
Therefore my heart is glad and my soul rejoices,
my body, too, abides in confidence
because you will not abandon my soul to the netherworld,
nor will you suffer your faithful one to undergo corruption.
R You are my inheritance, O Lord.
You will show me the path to life,
fullness of joys in your presence,
the delights at your right hand forever.
R You are my inheritance, O Lord.

What does the psalmist mean when he says the Lord is his inheritance?

A reading from the Letter of St. Paul to the Galatians

Gal 5:1, 13-18

Brothers and sisters:
For freedom Christ set us free;
so stand firm and do not submit again to the yoke of slavery.

For you were called for freedom, brothers and sisters.
But do not use this freedom
as an opportunity for the flesh;
rather, serve one another through love.
For the whole law is fulfilled in one statement,
namely, *You shall love your neighbor as yourself.*
But if you go on biting and devouring one another,
beware that you are not consumed by one another.

I say, then: live by the Spirit
and you will certainly not gratify the desire of the flesh.
For the flesh has desires against the Spirit,
and the Spirit against the flesh;
these are opposed to each other,
so that you may not do what you want.
But if you are guided by the Spirit, you are not under the law.

WHAT SORT of freedom does God offer, and how are we to use it responsibly?

A reading from the holy Gospel according to Luke

Lk 9:51-62

When the days for Jesus' being taken up were fulfilled,
he resolutely determined to journey to Jerusalem,
and he sent messengers ahead of him.
On the way they entered a Samaritan village
to prepare for his reception there,
but they would not welcome him
because the destination of his journey was Jerusalem.
When the disciples James and John saw this they asked,
"Lord, do you want us to call down fire from heaven
to consume them?"
Jesus turned and rebuked them, and they journeyed to another village.

As they were proceeding on their journey someone said to him,
"I will follow you wherever you go."
Jesus answered him,
"Foxes have dens and birds of the sky have nests,
but the Son of Man has nowhere to rest his head."

And to another he said, "Follow me."
But he replied, "Lord, let me go first and bury my father."
But he answered him, "Let the dead bury their dead.
But you, go and proclaim the kingdom of God."
And another said, "I will follow you, Lord,
but first let me say farewell to my family at home."
To him Jesus said, "No one who sets a hand to the plow
and looks to what was left behind is fit for the kingdom of God."

St. John of the Cross wrote of the principle of detachment, of letting go of earthly things that keep us from pursuing God. List an example of detachment from today's Gospel.

Pray:

Lord, help me to be attached only to those things which bring me closer to you. Amen.

Think:

God has given humanity free will. What is free will? How do you see it reflected in today's readings?

Go Forth:

Lent isn't the only time of the year you can give something up. This week, choose one thing you're very attached to (maybe a game? A book? An activity?) and go without it for one week.

OH LORD,
YOU HAVE
BEEN OUR
REFUGE
IN ALL
GENERATIONS.

-St. Boniface

4

FOURTEENTH SUNDAY IN ORDINARY TIME

A reading from the Book of the Prophet Isaiah
Is 66:10-14c

Thus says the LORD:
Rejoice with Jerusalem and be glad because of her,
all you who love her;
exult, exult with her,
all you who were mourning over her!
Oh, that you may suck fully
of the milk of her comfort,
that you may nurse with delight
at her abundant breasts!
For thus says the LORD:
Lo, I will spread prosperity over Jerusalem like a river,
and the wealth of the nations like an overflowing torrent.
As nurslings, you shall be carried in her arms,
and fondled in her lap;
as a mother comforts her child,
so will I comfort you;
in Jerusalem you shall find your comfort.

When you see this, your heart shall rejoice

and your bodies flourish like the grass;
the LORD's power shall be known to his servants.

ISAIAH COMPARES Jerusalem to a mother nurturing her child. Why do you think that is? Talk with your parents and your Pastor if you aren't sure.

Responsorial Psalm

Ps 66:1-3, 4-5, 6-7, 16, 20

R. (1) Let all the earth cry out to God with joy.
Shout joyfully to God, all the earth,
sing praise to the glory of his name;
proclaim his glorious praise.
Say to God, "How tremendous are your deeds!"
R. Let all the earth cry out to God with joy.
"Let all on earth worship and sing praise to you,
sing praise to your name!"
Come and see the works of God,
his tremendous deeds among the children of Adam.
R. Let all the earth cry out to God with joy.
He has changed the sea into dry land;
through the river they passed on foot;
therefore let us rejoice in him.
He rules by his might forever.
R. Let all the earth cry out to God with joy.
Hear now, all you who fear God, while I declare
what he has done for me.

Blessed be God who refused me not
my prayer or his kindness!
R. Let all the earth cry out to God with joy.

Today's psalm is a hymn of praise. Think back to the time you spend in prayer. How often do you praise God for his goodness?

A reading from the Letter of St. Paul to the Galatians

Gal 6:14-18

Brothers and sisters:
May I never boast except in the cross of our Lord Jesus Christ,
through which the world has been crucified to me,
and I to the world.
For neither does circumcision mean anything, nor does uncircumcision,
but only a new creation.
Peace and mercy be to all who follow this rule
and to the Israel of God.

From now on, let no one make troubles for me;
for I bear the marks of Jesus on my body.

The grace of our Lord Jesus Christ be with your spirit,
brothers and sisters. Amen.

WHAT DOES it mean to boast? What does St. Paul mean when he says, "May I never boast except in the cross of our Lord Jesus Christ?

A reading from the holy Gospel according to Luke

Lk 10:1-12, 17-20 (OR Lk 10:1-9)

At that time the Lord appointed seventy-two others
whom he sent ahead of him in pairs
to every town and place he intended to visit.
He said to them,
"The harvest is abundant but the laborers are few;
so ask the master of the harvest
to send out laborers for his harvest.
Go on your way;
behold, I am sending you like lambs among wolves.
Carry no money bag, no sack, no sandals;
and greet no one along the way.
Into whatever house you enter, first say,
'Peace to this household.'
If a peaceful person lives there,
your peace will rest on him;
but if not, it will return to you.
Stay in the same house and eat and drink what is offered to you,
for the laborer deserves his payment.
Do not move about from one house to another.
Whatever town you enter and they welcome you,
eat what is set before you,
cure the sick in it and say to them,
'The kingdom of God is at hand for you.'

Whatever town you enter and they do not receive you,
go out into the streets and say,
'The dust of your town that clings to our feet,
even that we shake off against you.'
Yet know this: the kingdom of God is at hand.
I tell you,
it will be more tolerable for Sodom on that day than for that town."

The seventy-two returned rejoicing, and said,
"Lord, even the demons are subject to us because of your name."
Jesus said, "I have observed Satan fall like lightning from the sky.
Behold, I have given you the power to 'tread upon serpents' and scorpions
and upon the full force of the enemy and nothing will harm you. Nevertheless, do
not rejoice because the spirits are subject to you,
but rejoice because your names are written in heaven."

RE-READ the last paragraph of today's Gospel, specifically on the words of guidance
Jesus offers to his apostles. What virtue is he encouraging them to show, and why?

Pray:

Heavenly Father, you are good and deserving of all my love. Help me to be humble.
Help me to praise you unceasingly. Help me to know, love, and serve you in this
world and the next. Amen.

Think:

What connection can you find between "boasting in the cross of Christ Jesus" and the virtue of humility?

Go Forth:

This week, practice saying short prayers of praise or gratitude. Every time something good happens, offer a silent prayer of thanksgiving to God.

THE FIRST DEGREE OF HUMILITY IS PROMPT OBEDIENCE.

-St. Benedict

5

FIFTEENTH SUNDAY IN ORDINARY TIME

 reading from the Book of Deuteronomy
Dt 30:10-14

Moses said to the people:
"If only you would heed the voice of the LORD, your God,
and keep his commandments and statutes
that are written in this book of the law,
when you return to the LORD, your God,
with all your heart and all your soul.

"For this command that I enjoin on you today
is not too mysterious and remote for you.
It is not up in the sky, that you should say,
'Who will go up in the sky to get it for us
and tell us of it, that we may carry it out?'
Nor is it across the sea, that you should say,
'Who will cross the sea to get it for us
and tell us of it, that we may carry it out?'
No, it is something very near to you,
already in your mouths and in your hearts;
you have only to carry it out."

MOSES OFFERS sage advice in today's reading from Deuteronomy. In the space below, take Moses' guidance and rewrite it in your own words.

Responsorial Psalm

Ps 69:14, 17, 30-31, 33-34, 36, 37 (OR Ps 19:8, 9, 10, 11)

R. (cf. 33) Turn to the Lord in your need, and you will live.
I pray to you, O LORD,
for the time of your favor, O God!
In your great kindness answer me
with your constant help.
Answer me, O LORD, for bounteous is your kindness:
in your great mercy turn toward me.
R. Turn to the Lord in your need, and you will live.
I am afflicted and in pain;
let your saving help, O God, protect me.
I will praise the name of God in song,
and I will glorify him with thanksgiving.
R. Turn to the Lord in your need, and you will live.
"See, you lowly ones, and be glad;
you who seek God, may your hearts revive!
For the LORD hears the poor,
and his own who are in bonds he spurns not."
R. Turn to the Lord in your need, and you will live.
For God will save Zion
and rebuild the cities of Judah.
The descendants of his servants shall inherit it,

and those who love his name shall inhabit it.
R. Turn to the Lord in your need, and you will live.

WHAT MIGHT it look like to turn to the Lord in your need? In other words, what are some ways you can turn to Him when you are struggling?

A reading from the Letter of St. Paul to the Colossians

Col 1:15-20

Christ Jesus is the image of the invisible God,
the firstborn of all creation.
For in him were created all things in heaven and on earth,
the visible and the invisible,
whether thrones or dominions or principalities or powers;
all things were created through him and for him.
He is before all things,
and in him all things hold together.
He is the head of the body, the church.
He is the beginning, the firstborn from the dead,
that in all things he himself might be preeminent.
For in him all the fullness was pleased to dwell,
and through him to reconcile all things for him,
making peace by the blood of his cross
through him, whether those on earth or those in heaven.

WHAT DOES it mean to say that Jesus is before all things? How does this apply in your own life?

A reading from the holy Gospel according to Luke

Lk 10:25-37

There was a scholar of the law who stood up to test Jesus and said,
"Teacher, what must I do to inherit eternal life?"
Jesus said to him, "What is written in the law?
How do you read it?"
He said in reply,
"You shall love the Lord, your God,
with all your heart,
with all your being,
with all your strength,
and with all your mind,
and your neighbor as yourself."
He replied to him, "You have answered correctly;
do this and you will live."

But because he wished to justify himself, he said to Jesus,
"And who is my neighbor?"
Jesus replied,
"A man fell victim to robbers
as he went down from Jerusalem to Jericho.
They stripped and beat him and went off leaving him half-dead.
A priest happened to be going down that road,
but when he saw him, he passed by on the opposite side.

Likewise a Levite came to the place,
and when he saw him, he passed by on the opposite side.
But a Samaritan traveler who came upon him
was moved with compassion at the sight.
He approached the victim,
poured oil and wine over his wounds and bandaged them.
Then he lifted him up on his own animal,
took him to an inn, and cared for him.
The next day he took out two silver coins
and gave them to the innkeeper with the instruction,
'Take care of him.
If you spend more than what I have given you,
I shall repay you on my way back.'
Which of these three, in your opinion,
was neighbor to the robbers' victim?"
He answered, "The one who treated him with mercy."
Jesus said to him, "Go and do likewise."

TODAY'S GOSPEL includes the parable of the Good Samaritan. With your parents' permission, take a few moments to research parables. What are they? Why did Jesus use them to teach? What insight does today's parable offer?

Pray:

Lord, sometimes I try to handle all my struggles and efforts on my own, without thinking of handing them over to you. St. Paul says that you are before all things; please help me remember to keep you first in everything that I do. Amen.

Think:

What does it mean to love your neighbor as yourself? Is it easy to do? Hard to do? Why?

Go Forth:

Think of one person you find hard to love. This week, make a special effort to serve this person through your words, thoughts, actions, and prayers.

HE LOVES. HE
HOPES. HE
WAITS. OUR
LORD PREFERS TO
WAIT HIMSELF FOR THE SINNER FOR YEARS
RATHER THAN
KEEP US WAITING
FOR AN INSTANT.
-St. Maria Goretti

6

SIXTEENTH SUNDAY IN ORDINARY TIME

 reading from the Book of Genesis
Gn 18:1-10a

The LORD appeared to Abraham by the terebinth of Mamre,
as he sat in the entrance of his tent,
while the day was growing hot.
Looking up, Abraham saw three men standing nearby.
When he saw them, he ran from the entrance of the tent to greet them;
and bowing to the ground, he said:
"Sir, if I may ask you this favor,
please do not go on past your servant.
Let some water be brought, that you may bathe your feet,
and then rest yourselves under the tree.
Now that you have come this close to your servant,
let me bring you a little food, that you may refresh yourselves;
and afterward you may go on your way."
The men replied, "Very well, do as you have said."

Abraham hastened into the tent and told Sarah,
"Quick, three measures of fine flour! Knead it and make rolls."
He ran to the herd, picked out a tender, choice steer,
and gave it to a servant, who quickly prepared it.

Then Abraham got some curds and milk,
as well as the steer that had been prepared,
and set these before the three men;
and he waited on them under the tree while they ate.

They asked Abraham, "Where is your wife Sarah?"
He replied, "There in the tent."
One of them said, "I will surely return to you about this time next year,
and Sarah will then have a son."

TODAY'S first reading doesn't identify the men who visit Abraham and Sarah. Based on the text of the reading, however, who do you think they are? Why?

Responsorial Psalm

Ps 15:2-3, 3-4, 5

R.(1a) He who does justice will live in the presence of the Lord.
One who walks blamelessly and does justice;
who thinks the truth in his heart
and slanders not with his tongue.
R. He who does justice will live in the presence of the Lord.
Who harms not his fellow man,
nor takes up a reproach against his neighbor;
by whom the reprobate is despised,
while he honors those who fear the LORD.
R. He who does justice will live in the presence of the Lord.

Who lends not his money at usury
and accepts no bribe against the innocent.
One who does these things
shall never be disturbed.
R. He who does justice will live in the presence of the Lord.

WHAT IS the virtue of justice? How does that definition differ from the secular sense of the word?

A reading from the Letter of St. Paul to the Colossians

Col 1:24-28

Brothers and sisters:
Now I rejoice in my sufferings for your sake,
and in my flesh I am filling up
what is lacking in the afflictions of Christ
on behalf of his body, which is the church,
of which I am a minister
in accordance with God's stewardship given to me
to bring to completion for you the word of God,
the mystery hidden from ages and from generations past.
But now it has been manifested to his holy ones,
to whom God chose to make known the riches of the glory
of this mystery among the Gentiles;
it is Christ in you, the hope for glory.
It is he whom we proclaim,

admonishing everyone and teaching everyone with all wisdom,
that we may present everyone perfect in Christ.

WHY DOES St. Paul rejoice in his sufferings? (Hint: think about it in the context of redemptive suffering)

A reading from the holy Gospel according to Luke

Lk 10:38-42

Jesus entered a village
where a woman whose name was Martha welcomed him.
She had a sister named Mary
who sat beside the Lord at his feet listening to him speak.
Martha, burdened with much serving, came to him and said,
"Lord, do you not care
that my sister has left me by myself to do the serving?
Tell her to help me."
The Lord said to her in reply,
"Martha, Martha, you are anxious and worried about many things.
There is need of only one thing.
Mary has chosen the better part
and it will not be taken from her."

THINK of a time when you probably could have related to Martha's frustration. How would Jesus' words to Martha apply in that situation for you?

Pray:

Heavenly Father, life is not without its difficulties and struggles, but I know that when I suffer well, I unite myself to your cross. Grant me the grace to rejoice in my sufferings, Lord, and offer them all to you. Amen.

Think:

You explored the definition of justice in the answer to the question on today's psalm. Compare and contrast the secular definition of justice with the true nature of justice as a virtue. How are they the same? How are they different?

Go Forth:

In what ways are you exhibiting the virtue of justice in your daily life? List some examples below, then add one or two more additional ideas.

TEACH US TO
GIVE AND
NOT TO
COUNT
THE COST
-St. Ignatius Loyola

7

SEVENTEENTH SUNDAY IN ORDINARY TIME

 reading from the Book of Genesis
Gn 18:20-32

In those days, the LORD said: "The outcry against Sodom and Gomorrah is so great, and their sin so grave,
that I must go down and see whether or not their actions
fully correspond to the cry against them that comes to me.
I mean to find out."

While Abraham's visitors walked on farther toward Sodom,
the LORD remained standing before Abraham.
Then Abraham drew nearer and said:
"Will you sweep away the innocent with the guilty?
Suppose there were fifty innocent people in the city;
would you wipe out the place, rather than spare it
for the sake of the fifty innocent people within it?
Far be it from you to do such a thing,
to make the innocent die with the guilty
so that the innocent and the guilty would be treated alike!
Should not the judge of all the world act with justice?"
The LORD replied,
"If I find fifty innocent people in the city of Sodom,

I will spare the whole place for their sake."
Abraham spoke up again:
"See how I am presuming to speak to my Lord,
though I am but dust and ashes!
What if there are five less than fifty innocent people?
Will you destroy the whole city because of those five?"
He answered, "I will not destroy it, if I find forty-five there."
But Abraham persisted, saying "What if only forty are found there?"
He replied, "I will forbear doing it for the sake of the forty."
Then Abraham said, "Let not my Lord grow impatient if I go on.
What if only thirty are found there?"
He replied, "I will forbear doing it if I can find but thirty there."
Still Abraham went on,
"Since I have thus dared to speak to my Lord,
what if there are no more than twenty?"
The LORD answered, "I will not destroy it, for the sake of the twenty."
But he still persisted:
"Please, let not my Lord grow angry if I speak up this last time.
What if there are at least ten there?"
He replied, "For the sake of those ten, I will not destroy it."

WHY DO you think Abraham petitions God to show mercy on the people of Sodom and Gomorrah?

Responsorial Psalm

Ps 138:1-2, 2-3, 6-7, 7-8

R.(3a) Lord, on the day I called for help, you answered me.
I will give thanks to you, O LORD, with all my heart,

for you have heard the words of my mouth;
in the presence of the angels I will sing your praise;
I will worship at your holy temple
and give thanks to your name.
R. Lord, on the day I called for help, you answered me.
Because of your kindness and your truth;
for you have made great above all things
your name and your promise.
When I called you answered me;
you built up strength within me.
R. Lord, on the day I called for help, you answered me.
The LORD is exalted, yet the lowly he sees,
and the proud he knows from afar.
Though I walk amid distress, you preserve me;
against the anger of my enemies you raise your hand.
R. Lord, on the day I called for help, you answered me.
Your right hand saves me.
The LORD will complete what he has done for me;
your kindness, O LORD, endures forever;
forsake not the work of your hands.
R. Lord, on the day I called for help, you answered me.

NAME A SAINT who might relate to the verses of today's Psalm. Explain your answer.

A reading of the Letter of St. Paul to the Colossians

Col 2:12-14

Brothers and sisters:
You were buried with him in baptism,
in which you were also raised with him
through faith in the power of God,
who raised him from the dead.
And even when you were dead
in transgressions and the uncircumcision of your flesh,
he brought you to life along with him,
having forgiven us all our transgressions;
obliterating the bond against us, with its legal claims,
which was opposed to us,
he also removed it from our midst, nailing it to the cross.

IN THE SPACE BELOW, rewrite this excerpt from St. Paul's Letter to the Colossians in your own words.

A reading from the Holy Gospel according to Luke

Lk 11:1-13

Jesus was praying in a certain place, and when he had finished,
one of his disciples said to him,
"Lord, teach us to pray just as John taught his disciples."
He said to them, "When you pray, say:

Father, hallowed be your name,
your kingdom come.
Give us each day our daily bread
and forgive us our sins
for we ourselves forgive everyone in debt to us,
and do not subject us to the final test."

And he said to them, "Suppose one of you has a friend
to whom he goes at midnight and says,
'Friend, lend me three loaves of bread,
for a friend of mine has arrived at my house from a journey
and I have nothing to offer him,'
and he says in reply from within,
'Do not bother me; the door has already been locked
and my children and I are already in bed.
I cannot get up to give you anything.'
I tell you,
if he does not get up to give the visitor the loaves
because of their friendship,
he will get up to give him whatever he needs
because of his persistence.

"And I tell you, ask and you will receive;
seek and you will find;
knock and the door will be opened to you.
For everyone who asks, receives;
and the one who seeks, finds;
and to the one who knocks, the door will be opened.
What father among you would hand his son a snake
when he asks for a fish?
Or hand him a scorpion when he asks for an egg?
If you then, who are wicked,
know how to give good gifts to your children,
how much more will the Father in heaven
give the Holy Spirit to those who ask him?"

IMAGINE a friend used this Gospel passage as proof that God will give you anything you request, so long as you ask for it. What would you say in response?

Pray:

Lord, align my will to yours. Help to me want only that which is good for me and in your holy plan. Amen.

Think:

What connection do you see between today's first reading from Genesis and the Gospel passage?

Go Forth:

Make a list of spiritual goals this week, specifically ways in which you would like to grow closer to the Lord.

I AM NOT MY
OWN.
I HAVE GIVEN MYSELF TO JESUS
-St. Kateri Tekawitha

8

EIGHTEENTH SUNDAY IN ORDINARY TIME

 reading from the Book of Ecclesiastes
Ecc 1:2; 2:21-23

Vanity of vanities, says Qoheleth,
vanity of vanities! All things are vanity!

Here is one who has labored with wisdom and knowledge and skill,
and yet to another who has not labored over it,
he must leave property.
This also is vanity and a great misfortune.
For what profit comes to man from all the toil and anxiety of heart
with which he has labored under the sun?
All his days sorrow and grief are his occupation;
even at night his mind is not at rest.
This also is vanity.

USING the text of the first reading, write a definition of the word vanity.

Responsorial Psalm

Ps 90:3-4, 5-6, 12-13, 14 and 17

R. (1) If today you hear his voice, harden not your hearts.
You turn man back to dust,
saying, "Return, O children of men."
For a thousand years in your sight
are as yesterday, now that it is past,
or as a watch of the night.
R. If today you hear his voice, harden not your hearts.
You make an end of them in their sleep;
the next morning they are like the changing grass,
Which at dawn springs up anew,
but by evening wilts and fades.
R. If today you hear his voice, harden not your hearts.
Teach us to number our days aright,
that we may gain wisdom of heart.
Return, O LORD! How long?
Have pity on your servants!
R. If today you hear his voice, harden not your hearts.
Fill us at daybreak with your kindness,
that we may shout for joy and gladness all our days.
And may the gracious care of the LORD our God be ours;
prosper the work of our hands for us!
Prosper the work of our hands!
R. If today you hear his voice, harden not your hearts.

WHAT DOES it mean to harden your heart against God's voice?

A reading from the Letter of St. Paul to the Colossians

Col 3:1-5, 9-11

Brothers and sisters:
If you were raised with Christ, seek what is above,
where Christ is seated at the right hand of God.
Think of what is above, not of what is on earth.
For you have died,
and your life is hidden with Christ in God.
When Christ your life appears,
then you too will appear with him in glory.

Put to death, then, the parts of you that are earthly:
immorality, impurity, passion, evil desire,
and the greed that is idolatry.
Stop lying to one another,
since you have taken off the old self with its practices
and have put on the new self,
which is being renewed, for knowledge,
in the image of its creator.
Here there is not Greek and Jew,
circumcision and uncircumcision,
barbarian, Scythian, slave, free;
but Christ is all and in all.

WHAT IS St. Paul encouraging the Colossians to do?

A reading from the holy Gospel according to Luke

Lk 12:13-21

Someone in the crowd said to Jesus,
"Teacher, tell my brother to share the inheritance with me."
He replied to him,
"Friend, who appointed me as your judge and arbitrator?"
Then he said to the crowd,
"Take care to guard against all greed,
for though one may be rich,
one's life does not consist of possessions."

Then he told them a parable.
"There was a rich man whose land produced a bountiful harvest.
He asked himself, 'What shall I do,
for I do not have space to store my harvest?'
And he said, 'This is what I shall do:
I shall tear down my barns and build larger ones.
There I shall store all my grain and other goods
and I shall say to myself, "Now as for you,
you have so many good things stored up for many years,
rest, eat, drink, be merry!"'
But God said to him,
'You fool, this night your life will be demanded of you;
and the things you have prepared, to whom will they belong?'
Thus will it be for all who store up treasure for themselves
but are not rich in what matters to God."

REMEMBER THE PRINCIPLE OF DETACHMENT? What connection can you make between it and today's Gospel?

Pray:

Increase my humility, Lord. Let me seek only to serve you, in my thoughts, in my words, and in my actions. Amen.

Think:

Why is it so hard for human beings to let go of material things? Remember, material things don't have to be objects. They can be habits and ideas, too.

Go Forth:

What material things are you holding onto that might be good to let go of? Try performing an examination of conscience at least twice this week and see if that helps you answer the question.

NOTHING IS
FAR FROM
GOD.
-St. Monica

9

NINETEENTH SUNDAY IN ORDINARY TIME

 reading from the Book of Wisdom
Wis 18:6-9

The night of the passover was known beforehand to our fathers,
that, with sure knowledge of the oaths in which they put their faith,
they might have courage.
Your people awaited the salvation of the just
and the destruction of their foes.
For when you punished our adversaries,
in this you glorified us whom you had summoned.
For in secret the holy children of the good were offering sacrifice
and putting into effect with one accord the divine institution.

HOW ARE the virtues of faith and fortitude (courage) connected to one another? In other words, how does faith increase fortitude, and vice versa?

Responsorial Psalm

Ps 33:1, 12, 18-19, 20-22

R. (12b) Blessed the people the Lord has chosen to be his own.B
Exult, you just, in the LORD;
praise from the upright is fitting.
Blessed the nation whose God is the LORD,
the people he has chosen for his own inheritance.
R. Blessed the people the Lord has chosen to be his own.
See, the eyes of the LORD are upon those who fear him,
upon those who hope for his kindness,
To deliver them from death
and preserve them in spite of famine.
R. Blessed the people the Lord has chosen to be his own.
Our soul waits for the LORD,
who is our help and our shield.
May your kindness, O LORD, be upon us
who have put our hope in you.
R. Blessed the people the Lord has chosen to be his own.

THE PSALMIST WRITES:

> Blessed the nation whose God is the LORD,
>   The people he has chosen for his own inheritance.

What is the Lord's inheritance as it is referred to here?

A reading from the Letter of St. Paul to the Hebrews

Heb 11:1-2, 8-19 (OR Heb 11:1-2, 8-12)

Brothers and sisters:
Faith is the realization of what is hoped for
and evidence of things not seen.
Because of it the ancients were well attested.

By faith Abraham obeyed when he was called to go out to a place
that he was to receive as an inheritance;
he went out, not knowing where he was to go.
By faith he sojourned in the promised land as in a foreign country,
dwelling in tents with Isaac and Jacob, heirs of the same promise;
for he was looking forward to the city with foundations,
whose architect and maker is God.
By faith he received power to generate,
even though he was past the normal age
—and Sarah herself was sterile—
for he thought that the one who had made the promise was
trustworthy.
So it was that there came forth from one man,
himself as good as dead,
descendants as numerous as the stars in the sky
and as countless as the sands on the seashore.

All these died in faith.
They did not receive what had been promised
but saw it and greeted it from afar
and acknowledged themselves to be strangers and aliens on earth,
for those who speak thus show that they are seeking a homeland.
If they had been thinking of the land from which they had come,
they would have had opportunity to return.
But now they desire a better homeland, a heavenly one.
Therefore, God is not ashamed to be called their God,
for he has prepared a city for them.

By faith Abraham, when put to the test, offered up Isaac,
and he who had received the promises was ready to offer his only son,
of whom it was said,

"Through Isaac descendants shall bear your name."
He reasoned that God was able to raise even from the dead,
and he received Isaac back as a symbol.

St. Paul gives the definition of faith at the beginning of this passage. How do his examples help support this definition?

A reading from the holy Gospel according to Luke

Lk 12:32-48 (OR Lk 12:35-40)

Jesus said to his disciples:
"Do not be afraid any longer, little flock,
for your Father is pleased to give you the kingdom.
Sell your belongings and give alms.
Provide money bags for yourselves that do not wear out,
an inexhaustible treasure in heaven
that no thief can reach nor moth destroy.
For where your treasure is, there also will your heart be.

"Gird your loins and light your lamps
and be like servants who await their master's return from a wedding,
ready to open immediately when he comes and knocks.
Blessed are those servants
whom the master finds vigilant on his arrival.
Amen, I say to you, he will gird himself,
have them recline at table, and proceed to wait on them.

And should he come in the second or third watch
and find them prepared in this way,
blessed are those servants.
Be sure of this:
if the master of the house had known the hour
when the thief was coming,
he would not have let his house be broken into.
You also must be prepared, for at an hour you do not expect,
the Son of Man will come."

Then Peter said,
"Lord, is this parable meant for us or for everyone?"
And the Lord replied,
"Who, then, is the faithful and prudent steward
whom the master will put in charge of his servants
to distribute the food allowance at the proper time?
Blessed is that servant whom his master on arrival finds doing so.
Truly, I say to you, the master will put the servant
in charge of all his property.
But if that servant says to himself,
'My master is delayed in coming,'
and begins to beat the menservants and the maidservants,
to eat and drink and get drunk,
then that servant's master will come
on an unexpected day and at an unknown hour
and will punish the servant severely
and assign him a place with the unfaithful.
That servant who knew his master's will
but did not make preparations nor act in accord with his will
shall be beaten severely;
and the servant who was ignorant of his master's will
but acted in a way deserving of a severe beating
shall be beaten only lightly.
Much will be required of the person entrusted with much,
and still more will be demanded of the person entrusted with more."

REWRITE the last sentence of today's Gospel in your own words. What does this statement mean for you?

Pray:

Heavenly Father, increase my faith. Help to trust you in all things, to be responsible with the gifts you have given me. Help me to be the person you want me to be. Amen.

Think:

Faith is a theme woven through today's readings. Which reading helped you understand the nature of faith the most, and why?

Go Forth:

This week, encourage your family to recite an Act of Faith together. You can find a prayer already composed or simply write one together as a family.

IN PRAYER,
MORE IS
ACCOMPLISHED BY
LISTENING
TALKING.
-St. Jane de Chantal

10

TWENTIETH SUNDAY IN ORDINARY TIME

A reading from the Book of the Prophet Jeremiah
Jer 38:4-6, 8-10

In those days, the princes said to the king:
"Jeremiah ought to be put to death;
he is demoralizing the soldiers who are left in this city,
and all the people, by speaking such things to them;
he is not interested in the welfare of our people,
but in their ruin."
King Zedekiah answered: "He is in your power";
for the king could do nothing with them.
And so they took Jeremiah
and threw him into the cistern of Prince Malchiah,
which was in the quarters of the guard,
letting him down with ropes.
There was no water in the cistern, only mud,
and Jeremiah sank into the mud.

Ebed-melech, a court official,
went there from the palace and said to him:
"My lord king,
these men have been at fault
in all they have done to the prophet Jeremiah,

casting him into the cistern.
He will die of famine on the spot,
for there is no more food in the city."
Then the king ordered Ebed-melech the Cushite
to take three men along with him,
and draw the prophet Jeremiah out of the cistern before he should die.

WHAT DOES Jeremiah's interaction with the King and the princes remind you of? Why?

Responsorial Psalm

Ps 40:2, 3, 4, 18
R. (14b) Lord, come to my aid!
I have waited, waited for the LORD,
and he stooped toward me.
R. Lord, come to my aid!
The LORD heard my cry.
He drew me out of the pit of destruction,
out of the mud of the swamp;
he set my feet upon a crag;
he made firm my steps.
R. Lord, come to my aid!
And he put a new song into my mouth,
a hymn to our God.
Many shall look on in awe
and trust in the LORD.

R. Lord, come to my aid!
Though I am afflicted and poor,
yet the LORD thinks of me.
You are my help and my deliverer;
O my God, hold not back!
R. Lord, come to my aid!

THINK of a time in your life where you needed to wait on God to answer your prayers. What was the experience of waiting like? What did you learn in the process?

A reading from the Letter of St. Paul to the Hebrews

Heb 12:1-4

Brothers and sisters:
Since we are surrounded by so great a cloud of witnesses,
let us rid ourselves of every burden and sin that clings to us
and persevere in running the race that lies before us
while keeping our eyes fixed on Jesus,
the leader and perfecter of faith.
For the sake of the joy that lay before him
he endured the cross, despising its shame,
and has taken his seat at the right of the throne of God.
Consider how he endured such opposition from sinners,
in order that you may not grow weary and lose heart.
In your struggle against sin
you have not yet resisted to the point of shedding blood.

St. Paul encourages the Hebrews to run the race with their eyes fixed on Christ. What is the race you are running? In other words, what journey of faith have you been on recently? How are you working to do as God desires?

A reading from the holy Gospel according to Luke

Lk 12:49-53

Jesus said to his disciples:
"I have come to set the earth on fire,
and how I wish it were already blazing!
There is a baptism with which I must be baptized,
and how great is my anguish until it is accomplished!
Do you think that I have come to establish peace on the earth?
No, I tell you, but rather division.
From now on a household of five will be divided,
three against two and two against three;
a father will be divided against his son
and a son against his father,
a mother against her daughter
and a daughter against her mother,
a mother-in-law against her daughter-in-law
and a daughter-in-law against her mother-in-law."

In what ways does Jesus sew division throughout his ministry? (Hint: did everybody like him? Why or why not?)

Pray:

Heavenly Father, I ask you to bless my family today. Bring us together in faith, love, and charity, that our efforts will always be directed toward you. Amen.

Think:

St. Paul writes of a great cloud of witnesses. To whom is he referring? If you could pick one example of great faith from the cloud of witnesses, who would it be and why?

Go Forth:

Set a spiritual goal for yourself this week. Will you try to pray a decade of the rosary every evening? Read Scripture every day before school? Be kind to a sibling or acquaintance who makes you want to pull your heart out? Write your goal here and record your progress throughout the week.

WE MUST
SEW THE
SEED
NOT HOARD IT.

-St. Dominic

11

SOLEMNITY OF THE ASSUMPTION OF THE BLESSED VIRGIN MARY

MASS DURING THE DAY

A reading from the Book of Revelation
RV 11:19A; 12:1-6A, 10AB

God's temple in heaven was opened,
and the ark of his covenant could be seen in the temple.

A great sign appeared in the sky, a woman clothed with the sun,
with the moon under her feet,
and on her head a crown of twelve stars.
She was with child and wailed aloud in pain as she labored to give birth.
Then another sign appeared in the sky;
it was a huge red dragon, with seven heads and ten horns,
and on its heads were seven diadems.
Its tail swept away a third of the stars in the sky
and hurled them down to the earth.
Then the dragon stood before the woman about to give birth,
to devour her child when she gave birth.
She gave birth to a son, a male child,
destined to rule all the nations with an iron rod.
Her child was caught up to God and his throne.
The woman herself fled into the desert
where she had a place prepared by God.

Then I heard a loud voice in heaven say:
"Now have salvation and power come,
and the Kingdom of our God
and the authority of his Anointed One."

THE BOOK of Revelation contains a great deal of symbolism, where objects can represent other things . What symbols do you see in this passage? What do they represent?

Responsorial Psalm

PS 45:10, 11, 12, 16

R. (10bc) The queen stands at your right hand, arrayed in gold.
The queen takes her place at your right hand in gold of Ophir.
R. The queen stands at your right hand, arrayed in gold.
Hear, O daughter, and see; turn your ear,
forget your people and your father's house.
R. The queen stands at your right hand, arrayed in gold.
So shall the king desire your beauty;
for he is your lord.
R. The queen stands at your right hand, arrayed in gold.
They are borne in with gladness and joy;
they enter the palace of the king.
R. The queen stands at your right hand, arrayed in gold.

WHAT MAKES this psalm appropriate for today's feast day?

A reading from the first Letter of St. Paul to the Corinthians

I COR 15:20-27

Brothers and sisters:
Christ has been raised from the dead,
the firstfruits of those who have fallen asleep.
For since death came through man,
the resurrection of the dead came also through man.
For just as in Adam all die,
so too in Christ shall all be brought to life,
but each one in proper order:
Christ the firstfruits;
then, at his coming, those who belong to Christ;
then comes the end,
when he hands over the Kingdom to his God and Father,
when he has destroyed every sovereignty
and every authority and power.
For he must reign until he has put all his enemies under his feet.
The last enemy to be destroyed is death,
for "he subjected everything under his feet."

WHAT IS St. Paul explaining to the Corinthians? How do you know?

A reading from the holy Gospel according to Luke

LK 1:39-56

Mary set out
and traveled to the hill country in haste
to a town of Judah,
where she entered the house of Zechariah
and greeted Elizabeth.
When Elizabeth heard Mary's greeting,
the infant leaped in her womb,
and Elizabeth, filled with the Holy Spirit,
cried out in a loud voice and said,
"Blessed are you among women,
and blessed is the fruit of your womb.
And how does this happen to me,
that the mother of my Lord should come to me?
For at the moment the sound of your greeting reached my ears,
the infant in my womb leaped for joy.
Blessed are you who believed
that what was spoken to you by the Lord
would be fulfilled."

And Mary said:
"My soul proclaims the greatness of the Lord;
my spirit rejoices in God my Savior
for he has looked with favor on his lowly servant.
From this day all generations will call me blessed:
the Almighty has done great things for me
and holy is his Name.
He has mercy on those who fear him
in every generation.
He has shown the strength of his arm,
and has scattered the proud in their conceit.
He has cast down the mighty from their thrones,
and has lifted up the lowly.
He has filled the hungry with good things,
and the rich he has sent away empty.
He has come to the help of his servant Israel

for he has remembered his promise of mercy,
the promise he made to our fathers,
to Abraham and his children forever."

Mary remained with her about three months
and then returned to her home.

WHICH CATHOLIC PRAYER is taken from this passage?

Pray:

Lord, thank you for the gift of the Blessed Virgin Mary. Help me to follow her example; the yes she gave to you in effort to do your will. Amen.

Think:

What is the significance of today's feast day?

Go Forth:

How would you explain the Catholic Church's stance on Mary to someone who doesn't understand why or how we honor her? Feel free to work with your parents on your answer.

[MARY] IS THE MOTHER OF MOTHERS.

SHE IS THE WORLD'S FIRST LOVE.

-Ven. Fulton Sheen

TWENTY-FIRST SUNDAY IN ORDINARY TIME

A reading from the Book of the Prophet Isaiah
Is 66:18-21

Thus says the LORD:
I know their works and their thoughts,
and I come to gather nations of every language;
they shall come and see my glory.
I will set a sign among them;
from them I will send fugitives to the nations:
to Tarshish, Put and Lud, Mosoch, Tubal and Javan,
to the distant coastlands
that have never heard of my fame, or seen my glory;
and they shall proclaim my glory among the nations.
They shall bring all your brothers and sisters from all the nations
as an offering to the LORD,
on horses and in chariots, in carts, upon mules and dromedaries,
to Jerusalem, my holy mountain, says the LORD,
just as the Israelites bring their offering
to the house of the LORD in clean vessels.
Some of these I will take as priests and Levites, says the LORD.

WHAT IS the Lord saying in this passage? Rewrite it in your own words below.

Responsorial Psalm

Ps 117:1, 2

R.(Mk 16:15) Go out to all the world and tell the Good News.
or:
R. Alleluia.
Praise the LORD all you nations;
glorify him, all you peoples!
R. Go out to all the world and tell the Good News.
or:
R. Alleluia.
For steadfast is his kindness toward us,
and the fidelity of the LORD endures forever.
R. Go out to all the world and tell the Good News.
or:
R. Alleluia.

LOOK up the definition of the word evangelization. How do you see evangelization reflected in today's Psalm?

A reading from the first Letter of St. Paul to the Hebrews

Heb 12:5-7, 11-13

Brothers and sisters,
You have forgotten the exhortation addressed to you as children:
"My son, do not disdain the discipline of the Lord
or lose heart when reproved by him;
for whom the Lord loves, he disciplines;
he scourges every son he acknowledges."
Endure your trials as "discipline";
God treats you as sons.
For what "son" is there whom his father does not discipline?
At the time,
all discipline seems a cause not for joy but for pain,
yet later it brings the peaceful fruit of righteousness
to those who are trained by it.

So strengthen your drooping hands and your weak knees.
Make straight paths for your feet,
that what is lame may not be disjointed but healed.

THE WORD DISCIPLINE has its roots in the word disciple. Does that change the way you view discipline? Why?

A reading from the holy Gospel according to Luke

Lk 13:22-30

Jesus passed through towns and villages,
teaching as he went and making his way to Jerusalem.
Someone asked him,
"Lord, will only a few people be saved?"
He answered them,
"Strive to enter through the narrow gate,
for many, I tell you, will attempt to enter
but will not be strong enough.
After the master of the house has arisen and locked the door,
then will you stand outside knocking and saying,
'Lord, open the door for us.'
He will say to you in reply,
'I do not know where you are from.
And you will say,
'We ate and drank in your company and you taught in our streets.'
Then he will say to you,
'I do not know where you are from.
Depart from me, all you evildoers!'
And there will be wailing and grinding of teeth
when you see Abraham, Isaac, and Jacob
and all the prophets in the kingdom of God
and you yourselves cast out.
And people will come from the east and the west
and from the north and the south
and will recline at table in the kingdom of God.
For behold, some are last who will be first,
and some are first who will be last."

JESUS OFTEN TURNS COMMONLY-HELD beliefs upside down. What human belief does he flip here, and why?

Pray:

Heavenly Father, make me a good disciple, both as a member of the body of Christ and as a member of my home. Make me humble, Lord, so that I might always seek what you want and not what I want. Amen.

Think:

Research the virtue of humility. How does it relate to today's readings?

Go Forth:

Talk to your parents about ways that you can be a better disciple in your home. What behaviors can you change? What acts of service can you increase? How can you help make your family a model of the Kingdom of God?

LET US STRIVE TO
PRAISE HIM
TO THE GREATEST
EXTENT OF OUR
POWERS.
-St. Maximillian Kolbe

13

TWENTY-SECOND SUNDAY IN ORDINARY TIME

 reading from the Book of Sirach
Sir 3:17-18, 20, 28-29

My child, conduct your affairs with humility,
and you will be loved more than a giver of gifts.
Humble yourself the more, the greater you are,
and you will find favor with God.
What is too sublime for you, seek not,
into things beyond your strength search not.
The mind of a sage appreciates proverbs,
and an attentive ear is the joy of the wise.
Water quenches a flaming fire,
and alms atone for sins.

WHY IS HUMILITY AN IMPORTANT VIRTUE? Include evidence from today's first reading in your answer.

Responsorial Psalm

Ps 68:4-5, 6-7, 10-11

R. (cf. 11b) God, in your goodness, you have made a home for the poor.
The just rejoice and exult before God;
they are glad and rejoice.
Sing to God, chant praise to his name;
whose name is the LORD.
R. God, in your goodness, you have made a home for the poor.
The father of orphans and the defender of widows
is God in his holy dwelling.
God gives a home to the forsaken;
he leads forth prisoners to prosperity.
R. God, in your goodness, you have made a home for the poor.
A bountiful rain you showered down, O God, upon your inheritance;
you restored the land when it languished;
your flock settled in it;
in your goodness, O God, you provided it for the needy.
R. God, in your goodness, you have made a home for the poor.

WHAT GROUPS of people are mentioned in today's Psalm? How do they exhibit humility?

A reading from the Letter of St. Paul to the Hebrews

Heb 12:18-19, 22-24a

Brothers and sisters:
You have not approached that which could be touched
and a blazing fire and gloomy darkness
and storm and a trumpet blast
and a voice speaking words such that those who heard
begged that no message be further addressed to them.
No, you have approached Mount Zion
and the city of the living God, the heavenly Jerusalem,
and countless angels in festal gathering,
and the assembly of the firstborn enrolled in heaven,
and God the judge of all,
and the spirits of the just made perfect,
and Jesus, the mediator of a new covenant,
and the sprinkled blood that speaks more eloquently than that of Abel.

WITH YOUR PARENTS' permission, research Mount Zion. What is it? Why does St. Paul
mention it here in his Letter to the Hebrews?

A reading from the holy Gospel according to Luke

Lk 14:1, 7-14

On a sabbath Jesus went to dine
at the home of one of the leading Pharisees,

and the people there were observing him carefully.

He told a parable to those who had been invited,
noticing how they were choosing the places of honor at the table.
"When you are invited by someone to a wedding banquet,
do not recline at table in the place of honor.
A more distinguished guest than you may have been invited by him,
and the host who invited both of you may approach you and say,
'Give your place to this man,'
and then you would proceed with embarrassment
to take the lowest place.
Rather, when you are invited,
go and take the lowest place
so that when the host comes to you he may say,
'My friend, move up to a higher position.'
Then you will enjoy the esteem of your companions at the table.
For every one who exalts himself will be humbled,
but the one who humbles himself will be exalted."
Then he said to the host who invited him,
"When you hold a lunch or a dinner,
do not invite your friends or your brothers
or your relatives or your wealthy neighbors,
in case they may invite you back and you have repayment.
Rather, when you hold a banquet,
invite the poor, the crippled, the lame, the blind;
blessed indeed will you be because of their inability to repay you.
For you will be repaid at the resurrection of the righteous."

IN WHAT WAY is the parable in today's Gospel an example of humility?

Pray:

Lord, there are days when I am too proud. When I don't want to be wrong. When I don't want to be last. When I don't want to be told what to do. Help me to turn to you during those moments. To rely on you and be humble for your sake, so that I might unite my sufferings to yours as you suffered on the Cross. Amen.

Think:

What saint is a good example of humility? How does this saint exemplify that virtue?

Go Forth:

What does humility look like for you? Are there ways in which you could work to be more humble? What are they?

TO DO
PENANCE IS
TO BEWAIL
THE EVIL WE
HAVE DONE
AND DO NO
EVIL TO
BEWAIL
-St. Gregory the Great

14

TWENTY-THIRD SUNDAY IN ORDINARY TIME

A reading from the Book of Wisdom

Wis 9:13-18b

Who can know God's counsel,
or who can conceive what the LORD intends?
For the deliberations of mortals are timid,
and unsure are our plans.
For the corruptible body burdens the soul
and the earthen shelter weighs down the mind that has many concerns.
And scarce do we guess the things on earth,
and what is within our grasp we find with difficulty;
but when things are in heaven, who can search them out?
Or who ever knew your counsel, except you had given wisdom
and sent your holy spirit from on high?
And thus were the paths of those on earth made straight.

TODAY'S first reading asks a good question: how can we know what God wants? If someone were to ask you this question, what would you say?

Responsorial Psalm

Ps 90:3-4, 5-6, 12-13, 14 and 17

R. (1) In every age, O Lord, you have been our refuge.
You turn man back to dust,
saying, "Return, O children of men."
For a thousand years in your sight
are as yesterday, now that it is past,
or as a watch of the night.
R. In every age, O Lord, you have been our refuge.
You make an end of them in their sleep;
the next morning they are like the changing grass,
Which at dawn springs up anew,
but by evening wilts and fades.
R. In every age, O Lord, you have been our refuge.
Teach us to number our days aright,
that we may gain wisdom of heart.
Return, O LORD! How long?
Have pity on your servants!
R. In every age, O Lord, you have been our refuge.
Fill us at daybreak with your kindness,
that we may shout for joy and gladness all our days.
And may the gracious care of the LORD our God be ours;
prosper the work of our hands for us!
Prosper the work of our hands!
R. In every age, O Lord, you have been our refuge.

How is the Lord your refuge? In what ways does he offer you comfort?

A reading from the Letter of St. Paul to Philemon

Phmn 9-10, 12-17

I, Paul, an old man,
and now also a prisoner for Christ Jesus,
urge you on behalf of my child Onesimus,
whose father I have become in my imprisonment;
I am sending him, that is, my own heart, back to you.
I should have liked to retain him for myself,
so that he might serve me on your behalf
in my imprisonment for the gospel,
but I did not want to do anything without your consent,
so that the good you do might not be forced but voluntary.
Perhaps this is why he was away from you for a while,
that you might have him back forever,
no longer as a slave
but more than a slave, a brother,
beloved especially to me, but even more so to you,
as a man and in the Lord.
So if you regard me as a partner, welcome him as you would me.

What is St. Paul asking of Philemon? Do you see any parallels between St. Paul sending Onesimus to Philemon and God the Father sending His Son to mankind?

∿

A reading from the Holy Gospel according to Luke

Lk 14:25-33

Great crowds were traveling with Jesus,
and he turned and addressed them,
"If anyone comes to me without hating his father and mother,
wife and children, brothers and sisters,
and even his own life,
he cannot be my disciple.
Whoever does not carry his own cross and come after me
cannot be my disciple.
Which of you wishing to construct a tower
does not first sit down and calculate the cost
to see if there is enough for its completion?
Otherwise, after laying the foundation
and finding himself unable to finish the work
the onlookers should laugh at him and say,
'This one began to build but did not have the resources to finish.'
Or what king marching into battle would not first sit down
and decide whether with ten thousand troops
he can successfully oppose another king
advancing upon him with twenty thousand troops?
But if not, while he is still far away,
he will send a delegation to ask for peace terms.
In the same way,
anyone of you who does not renounce all his possessions
cannot be my disciple."

WHY IS it necessary to pick up our cross and let go of earthly attachments if we are truly going to follow Jesus?

∾

Pray:

Lord, grant me wisdom. Grant me the ability to hear your voice, so that I might know what path to take when I am faced with a decision. Help me to let go of earthly attachments and rest in you, knowing that you will always provide for me. Amen.

Think:

What crosses have you experienced that have brought you closer to God? In other words, what struggles or difficulties have you faced that helped you grow in grace and wisdom?

Go Forth:

A few weeks ago, we talked about the principle of detachment: letting go of earthly desires in order to focus more completely on God. This week, do a little detachment check-in. What earthly desires might you need to let go of? Why?

SERVE THE LORD
WITH
LAUGHTER

-Padre Pio

15

TWENTY-FOURTH SUNDAY IN ORDINARY TIME

A reading from the Book of Exodus
Ex 32:7-11, 13-14

The LORD said to Moses,
"Go down at once to your people,
whom you brought out of the land of Egypt,
for they have become depraved.
They have soon turned aside from the way I pointed out to them,
making for themselves a molten calf and worshiping it,
sacrificing to it and crying out,
'This is your God, O Israel,
who brought you out of the land of Egypt!'
"I see how stiff-necked this people is," continued the LORD to Moses.
Let me alone, then,
that my wrath may blaze up against them to consume them.
Then I will make of you a great nation."

But Moses implored the LORD, his God, saying,
"Why, O LORD, should your wrath blaze up against your own people,
whom you brought out of the land of Egypt
with such great power and with so strong a hand?
Remember your servants Abraham, Isaac, and Israel,
and how you swore to them by your own self, saying,

'I will make your descendants as numerous as the stars in the sky;
and all this land that I promised,
I will give your descendants as their perpetual heritage.'"
So the LORD relented in the punishment
he had threatened to inflict on his people.

ARE you surprised that Moses implored God to show mercy to the people of Israel?
Why or why not?

Responsorial Psalm

Ps 51:3-4, 12-13, 17, 19

R. (Lk 15:18) I will rise and go to my father.
Have mercy on me, O God, in your goodness;
in the greatness of your compassion wipe out my offense.
Thoroughly wash me from my guilt
and of my sin cleanse me.
R. I will rise and go to my father.
A clean heart create for me, O God,
and a steadfast spirit renew within me.
Cast me not out from your presence,
and your Holy Spirit take not from me.
R. I will rise and go to my father.
O Lord, open my lips,
and my mouth shall proclaim your praise.
My sacrifice, O God, is a contrite spirit;
a heart contrite and humbled, O God, you will not spurn.

R. I will rise and go to my father.

How is God's mercy reflected in today's Psalm?

A reading from the first Letter of St. Paul to Timothy

1 Tm 1:12-17

Beloved:
I am grateful to him who has strengthened me, Christ Jesus our Lord,
because he considered me trustworthy
in appointing me to the ministry.
I was once a blasphemer and a persecutor and arrogant,
but I have been mercifully treated
because I acted out of ignorance in my unbelief.
Indeed, the grace of our Lord has been abundant,
along with the faith and love that are in Christ Jesus.
This saying is trustworthy and deserves full acceptance:
Christ Jesus came into the world to save sinners.
Of these I am the foremost.
But for that reason I was mercifully treated,
so that in me, as the foremost,
Christ Jesus might display all his patience as an example
for those who would come to believe in him for everlasting life.
To the king of ages, incorruptible, invisible, the only God,
honor and glory forever and ever. Amen.

WHAT REASON DOES St. Paul give for God's mercy upon him? In other words, how has St. Paul changed his life and used it differently after receiving God's merciful grace?

A reading from the holy Gospel according to Luke

Lk 15:1-32 (OR Lk 15:1-10)

Tax collectors and sinners were all drawing near to listen to Jesus,
but the Pharisees and scribes began to complain, saying,
"This man welcomes sinners and eats with them."
So to them he addressed this parable.
"What man among you having a hundred sheep and losing one of them
would not leave the ninety-nine in the desert
and go after the lost one until he finds it?
And when he does find it,
he sets it on his shoulders with great joy
and, upon his arrival home,
he calls together his friends and neighbors and says to them,
'Rejoice with me because I have found my lost sheep.'
I tell you, in just the same way
there will be more joy in heaven over one sinner who repents
than over ninety-nine righteous people
who have no need of repentance.

"Or what woman having ten coins and losing one
would not light a lamp and sweep the house,
searching carefully until she finds it?
And when she does find it,
she calls together her friends and neighbors

and says to them,
'Rejoice with me because I have found the coin that I lost.'
In just the same way, I tell you,
there will be rejoicing among the angels of God
over one sinner who repents."

Then he said,
"A man had two sons, and the younger son said to his father,
'Father give me the share of your estate that should come to me.'
So the father divided the property between them.
After a few days, the younger son collected all his belongings
and set off to a distant country
where he squandered his inheritance on a life of dissipation.
When he had freely spent everything,
a severe famine struck that country,
and he found himself in dire need.
So he hired himself out to one of the local citizens
who sent him to his farm to tend the swine.
And he longed to eat his fill of the pods on which the swine fed,
but nobody gave him any.
Coming to his senses he thought,
'How many of my father's hired workers
have more than enough food to eat,
but here am I, dying from hunger.
I shall get up and go to my father and I shall say to him,
"Father, I have sinned against heaven and against you.
I no longer deserve to be called your son;
treat me as you would treat one of your hired workers."'
So he got up and went back to his father.
While he was still a long way off,
his father caught sight of him,
and was filled with compassion.
He ran to his son, embraced him and kissed him.
His son said to him,
'Father, I have sinned against heaven and against you;
I no longer deserve to be called your son.'
But his father ordered his servants,
'Quickly bring the finest robe and put it on him;
put a ring on his finger and sandals on his feet.
Take the fattened calf and slaughter it.

Then let us celebrate with a feast,
because this son of mine was dead, and has come to life again;
he was lost, and has been found.'
Then the celebration began.
Now the older son had been out in the field
and, on his way back, as he neared the house,
he heard the sound of music and dancing.
He called one of the servants and asked what this might mean.
The servant said to him,
'Your brother has returned
and your father has slaughtered the fattened calf
because he has him back safe and sound.'
He became angry,
and when he refused to enter the house,
his father came out and pleaded with him.
He said to his father in reply,
'Look, all these years I served you
and not once did I disobey your orders;
yet you never gave me even a young goat to feast on with my friends. But when your
son returns,
who swallowed up your property with prostitutes,
for him you slaughter the fattened calf.'
He said to him,
'My son, you are here with me always;
everything I have is yours.
But now we must celebrate and rejoice,
because your brother was dead and has come to life again;
he was lost and has been found.'"

WHAT LESSON CAN you learn from the parable of the Prodigal Son? Not just from the
way the prodigal son is received by his father, but also the way the father responds to
the son who stayed and served his father well?

Pray:

Heavenly Father, you are good and all merciful. Help me to seek your mercy day in and day out, to seek your grace as a necessary and vital part of my life in Christ. Amen.

Think:

Why is God's mercy so amazing? What are some ways in which you can experience God's mercy in your life?

Go Forth:

This week, take time to do an examination of conscience. If you haven't been to confession in a while, ask your parents to take you some time this week.

CHARITY
IS THAT WITH
WHICH NO MAN
IS LOST, AND
WITHOUT WHICH
NO MAN IS
SAVED.

-St. Robert Bellarmine

16

TWENTY-FIFTH SUNDAY IN ORDINARY TIME

A reading from the Book of the Prophet Amos
Am 8:4-7

Hear this, you who trample upon the needy
and destroy the poor of the land!
"When will the new moon be over," you ask,
"that we may sell our grain,
and the sabbath, that we may display the wheat?
We will diminish the ephah,
add to the shekel,
and fix our scales for cheating!
We will buy the lowly for silver,
and the poor for a pair of sandals;
even the refuse of the wheat we will sell!"
The LORD has sworn by the pride of Jacob:
Never will I forget a thing they have done!

WHAT DOES Amos tell those who seek to do evil? What will the Lord do in response?

Responsorial Psalm

Ps 113:1-2, 4-6, 7-8

R. (cf. 1a, 7b) Praise the Lord who lifts up the poor.
or:
R. Alleluia.
Praise, you servants of the LORD,
praise the name of the LORD.
Blessed be the name of the LORD
both now and forever.
R. Praise the Lord who lifts up the poor.
or:
R. Alleluia.
High above all nations is the LORD;
above the heavens is his glory.
Who is like the LORD, our God, who is enthroned on high
and looks upon the heavens and the earth below?
R. Praise the Lord who lifts up the poor.
or:
R. Alleluia.
He raises up the lowly from the dust;
from the dunghill he lifts up the poor
to seat them with princes,
with the princes of his own people.
R. Praise the Lord who lifts up the poor.
or:
R. Alleluia.

REWRITE the message of today's Psalm below in your own words.

A reading from the first Letter of St. Paul to Timothy

1 Tm 2:1-8

Beloved:
First of all, I ask that supplications, prayers,
petitions, and thanksgivings be offered for everyone,
for kings and for all in authority,
that we may lead a quiet and tranquil life
in all devotion and dignity.
This is good and pleasing to God our savior,
who wills everyone to be saved
and to come to knowledge of the truth.
For there is one God.
There is also one mediator between God and men,
the man Christ Jesus,
who gave himself as ransom for all.
This was the testimony at the proper time.
For this I was appointed preacher and apostle
— I am speaking the truth, I am not lying —,
teacher of the Gentiles in faith and truth.

It is my wish, then, that in every place the men should pray,
lifting up holy hands, without anger or argument.

WHAT DOES St. Paul mean when he says Jesus gave himself as ransom for all?

A reading from the holy Gospel according to Luke

Lk 16:1-13 (OR Lk 16:10-13)

Jesus said to his disciples,
"A rich man had a steward
who was reported to him for squandering his property.
He summoned him and said,
'What is this I hear about you?
Prepare a full account of your stewardship,
because you can no longer be my steward.'
The steward said to himself, 'What shall I do,
now that my master is taking the position of steward away from me?
I am not strong enough to dig and I am ashamed to beg.
I know what I shall do so that,
when I am removed from the stewardship,
they may welcome me into their homes.'
He called in his master's debtors one by one.
To the first he said,
'How much do you owe my master?'
He replied, 'One hundred measures of olive oil.'
He said to him, 'Here is your promissory note.
Sit down and quickly write one for fifty.'
Then to another the steward said, 'And you, how much do you owe?'
He replied, 'One hundred kors of wheat.'
The steward said to him, 'Here is your promissory note;
write one for eighty.'
And the master commended that dishonest steward for acting prudently.
"For the children of this world
are more prudent in dealing with their own generation
than are the children of light.
I tell you, make friends for yourselves with dishonest wealth,
so that when it fails, you will be welcomed into eternal dwellings.
The person who is trustworthy in very small matters
is also trustworthy in great ones;
and the person who is dishonest in very small matters
is also dishonest in great ones.
If, therefore, you are not trustworthy with dishonest wealth,
who will trust you with true wealth?
If you are not trustworthy with what belongs to another,

who will give you what is yours?
No servant can serve two masters.
He will either hate one and love the other,
or be devoted to one and despise the other.
You cannot serve both God and mammon."

WHY IS hard to serve both God and the secular world? What does this mean for those of us who are called to be in the world but not of it?

Pray:

Heavenly Father, I want to serve you. I want to love, know, and serve you in this world and the next. Cover me in your graces, Lord, so that I might seek your grace and your mercy. Help me to devote my heart to you. Amen.

Think:

Did you notice a theme in today's readings? What was it? Use specific details from the scripture passages to support your answer.

Go Forth:

Review the corporal and spiritual works of mercy. Choose one corporal work of mercy and one spiritual work of mercy and perform them both this week.

SEEK GOOD IN
ALL THINGS AND
YOU SHALL

FIND GOD AT YOUR SIDE.

-St. Peter Claver

17

TWENTY-SIXTH SUNDAY IN ORDINARY TIME

A reading from the Book of the Prophet Amos
Am 6:1a, 4-7

Thus says the LORD the God of hosts:
Woe to the complacent in Zion!
Lying upon beds of ivory,
stretched comfortably on their couches,
they eat lambs taken from the flock,
and calves from the stall!
Improvising to the music of the harp,
like David, they devise their own accompaniment.
They drink wine from bowls
and anoint themselves with the best oils;
yet they are not made ill by the collapse of Joseph!
Therefore, now they shall be the first to go into exile,
and their wanton revelry shall be done away with.

WHAT DOES it mean to be complacent? Why is complacency a dangerous attitude?

Responsorial Psalm

Ps 146:7, 8-9, 9-10

R. (1b) Praise the Lord, my soul!
or:
R. Alleluia.
Blessed he who keeps faith forever,
secures justice for the oppressed,
gives food to the hungry.
The LORD sets captives free.
R. Praise the Lord, my soul!
or:
R. Alleluia.
The LORD gives sight to the blind;
the LORD raises up those who were bowed down.
The LORD loves the just;
the LORD protects strangers.
R. Praise the Lord, my soul!
or:
R. Alleluia.
The fatherless and the widow he sustains,
but the way of the wicked he thwarts.
The LORD shall reign forever;
your God, O Zion, through all generations. Alleluia.
R. Praise the Lord, my soul!
or:
R. Alleluia.

WHY IS it important to offer praise to God? What are some ways in which we can offer Him praise on a daily basis, in addition to prayer?

A reading from the first Letter of St. Paul to Timothy

1 Tm 6:11-16

But you, man of God, pursue righteousness,
devotion, faith, love, patience, and gentleness.
Compete well for the faith.
Lay hold of eternal life, to which you were called
when you made the noble confession in the presence of many witnesses.
I charge you before God, who gives life to all things,
and before Christ Jesus,
who gave testimony under Pontius Pilate for the noble confession,
to keep the commandment without stain or reproach
until the appearance of our Lord Jesus Christ
that the blessed and only ruler
will make manifest at the proper time,
the King of kings and Lord of lords,
who alone has immortality, who dwells in unapproachable light,
and whom no human being has seen or can see.
To him be honor and eternal power. Amen.

WHY DO you think St. Paul wrote to individuals like Timothy and communities like the Galatians and the Colossians? What do his letters offer to those whom he is writing?

A reading from the holy Gospel according to Luke

Lk 16:19-31

Jesus said to the Pharisees:
"There was a rich man who dressed in purple garments and fine linen
and dined sumptuously each day.
And lying at his door was a poor man named Lazarus, covered with sores,
who would gladly have eaten his fill of the scraps
that fell from the rich man's table.
Dogs even used to come and lick his sores.
When the poor man died,
he was carried away by angels to the bosom of Abraham.
The rich man also died and was buried,
and from the netherworld, where he was in torment,
he raised his eyes and saw Abraham far off
and Lazarus at his side.
And he cried out, 'Father Abraham, have pity on me.
Send Lazarus to dip the tip of his finger in water and cool my tongue,
for I am suffering torment in these flames.'
Abraham replied,
'My child, remember that you received
what was good during your lifetime
while Lazarus likewise received what was bad;
but now he is comforted here, whereas you are tormented.
Moreover, between us and you a great chasm is established
to prevent anyone from crossing who might wish to go
from our side to yours or from your side to ours.'
He said, 'Then I beg you, father,
send him to my father's house, for I have five brothers,
so that he may warn them,
lest they too come to this place of torment.'
But Abraham replied, 'They have Moses and the prophets.
Let them listen to them.'
He said, 'Oh no, father Abraham,
but if someone from the dead goes to them, they will repent.'
Then Abraham said, 'If they will not listen to Moses and the prophets,
neither will they be persuaded if someone should rise from the dead.'"

READ back through today's Gospel. Which line or lines stand out to you? Why?

Pray:

Lord, light a fire in my soul. Let me be on fire for you and your glory. Protect me from complacency and ignite a true desire to unify my will with yours. Amen

Think:

What makes people turn away from God? Is it a sudden turn? Or do you think it's more gradual? Why?

Go Forth:

What areas of your spiritual life could use a little boost? Are you getting distracted during prayer time? Has it been easier to zone out during Mass? Has it been a while since you've been to confession? What are some ways you can give your faith a boost?

THE WORLD'S
THY SHIP
AND NOT
THY HOME.

-St. Therese of Lisieux

18

TWENTY-SEVENTH SUNDAY IN ORDINARY TIME

A reading from the Book of Habakkuk
Hab 1:2-3; 2:2-4

How long, O LORD? I cry for help
but you do not listen!
I cry out to you, "Violence!"
but you do not intervene.
Why do you let me see ruin;
why must I look at misery?
Destruction and violence are before me;
there is strife, and clamorous discord.
Then the LORD answered me and said:
Write down the vision clearly upon the tablets,
so that one can read it readily.
For the vision still has its time,
presses on to fulfillment, and will not disappoint;
if it delays, wait for it,
it will surely come, it will not be late.
The rash one has no integrity;
but the just one, because of his faith, shall live.

WHY DOES God sometimes not answer our prayers? Include your parents in the discussion of your answer.

Responsorial Psalm

Ps 95:1-2, 6-7, 8-9

R. (8) If today you hear his voice, harden not your hearts.
Come, let us sing joyfully to the LORD;
let us acclaim the Rock of our salvation.
Let us come into his presence with thanksgiving;
let us joyfully sing psalms to him.
R. If today you hear his voice, harden not your hearts.
Come, let us bow down in worship;
let us kneel before the LORD who made us.
For he is our God,
and we are the people he shepherds, the flock he guides.
R. If today you hear his voice, harden not your hearts.
Oh, that today you would hear his voice:
"Harden not your hearts as at Meribah,
as in the day of Massah in the desert,
Where your fathers tempted me;
they tested me though they had seen my works."
R. If today you hear his voice, harden not your hearts.

List three ways you can soften your heart toward God. What activities or reading might help you hear God's voice and do his will?

A reading from the second Letter of St. Paul to Timothy

2 Tm 1:6-8, 13-14

Beloved:
I remind you, to stir into flame
the gift of God that you have through the imposition of my hands.
For God did not give us a spirit of cowardice
but rather of power and love and self-control.
So do not be ashamed of your testimony to our Lord,
nor of me, a prisoner for his sake;
but bear your share of hardship for the gospel
with the strength that comes from God.

Take as your norm the sound words that you heard from me,
in the faith and love that are in Christ Jesus.
Guard this rich trust with the help of the Holy Spirit
that dwells within us.

WHAT VERSE OR verses stood out to you the most? Why?

A reading from the holy Gospel according to Luke

Lk 17:5-10

The apostles said to the Lord, "Increase our faith."
The Lord replied,
"If you have faith the size of a mustard seed,

you would say to this mulberry tree,
'Be uprooted and planted in the sea,' and it would obey you.

"Who among you would say to your servant
who has just come in from plowing or tending sheep in the field,
'Come here immediately and take your place at table'?
Would he not rather say to him,
'Prepare something for me to eat.
Put on your apron and wait on me while I eat and drink.
You may eat and drink when I am finished'?
Is he grateful to that servant because he did what was commanded?
So should it be with you.
When you have done all you have been commanded,
say, 'We are unprofitable servants;
we have done what we were obliged to do.'"

WITH YOUR PARENTS' permission, research the size of a mustard seed. How does that change your understanding of the reading?

Pray:

Heavenly Father, increase my faith. Help me to trust in you and believe in you always, without question, especially in situations that might cause me to doubt. Amen.

Think:

Look back at the second stanza in today's Gospel. What is Jesus saying, and why?

Go Forth:

Talk with your family this week about what faith means. How can you grow in faith together?

LET US LOVE SILENCE
UNTIL THE WORLD
IS MADE TO DIE IN
OUR HEARTS.
-St. Isaac Jogues

19

TWENTY-EIGHTH SUNDAY IN ORDINARY TIME

 reading from the second Book of Kings
2 Kgs 5:14-17

Naaman went down and plunged into the Jordan seven times
at the word of Elisha, the man of God.
His flesh became again like the flesh of a little child,
and he was clean of his leprosy.

Naaman returned with his whole retinue to the man of God.
On his arrival he stood before Elisha and said,
"Now I know that there is no God in all the earth,
except in Israel.
Please accept a gift from your servant."

Elisha replied, "As the LORD lives whom I serve, I will not take it;"
and despite Naaman's urging, he still refused.
Naaman said: "If you will not accept,
please let me, your servant, have two mule-loads of earth,
for I will no longer offer holocaust or sacrifice
to any other god except to the LORD."

WHY DO you think Elisha refuses Naaman's gift? (Hint: think about humility. Could that have something to do with it?)

Responsorial Psalm

Ps 98:1, 2-3, 3-4

R. (cf. 2b) The Lord has revealed to the nations his saving power.
Sing to the LORD a new song,
for he has done wondrous deeds;
his right hand has won victory for him,
his holy arm.
R. The Lord has revealed to the nations his saving power.
The LORD has made his salvation known:
in the sight of the nations he has revealed his justice.
He has remembered his kindness and his faithfulness
toward the house of Israel.
R. The Lord has revealed to the nations his saving power.
All the ends of the earth have seen
the salvation by our God.
Sing joyfully to the LORD, all you lands:
break into song; sing praise.
R. The Lord has revealed to the nations his saving power.

WHAT IS God's saving power and how can we see it?

A reading from the second Letter of St. Paul to Timothy

2 Tm 2:8-13

Beloved: Remember Jesus Christ, raised from the dead, a descendant of David: such is my gospel, for which I am suffering, even to the point of chains, like a criminal. But the word of God is not chained. Therefore, I bear with everything for the sake of those who are chosen, so that they too may obtain the salvation that is in Christ Jesus, together with eternal glory. This saying is trustworthy:

If we have died with him
we shall also live with him;
if we persevere
we shall also reign with him.
But if we deny him
he will deny us.
If we are unfaithful
he remains faithful,
for he cannot deny himself.

WHY IS St. Paul willing to accept imprisonment in order to share the Gospel with those who have not yet heard it?

A reading from the holy Gospel according to Luke

Lk 17:11-19

As Jesus continued his journey to Jerusalem,
he traveled through Samaria and Galilee.
As he was entering a village, ten lepers met him.
They stood at a distance from him and raised their voices, saying,
"Jesus, Master! Have pity on us!"
And when he saw them, he said,
"Go show yourselves to the priests."
As they were going they were cleansed.
And one of them, realizing he had been healed,
returned, glorifying God in a loud voice;
and he fell at the feet of Jesus and thanked him.
He was a Samaritan.
Jesus said in reply,
"Ten were cleansed, were they not?
Where are the other nine?
Has none but this foreigner returned to give thanks to God?"
Then he said to him, "Stand up and go;
your faith has saved you."

WHY DOES the Samaritan come back to thank Jesus for his healing?

Pray:

Lord, gratitude is difficult. It is sometimes easier to go about my day without thinking
of the ways in which my family and I have been blessed. You have given us so much.
Thank you for blessing my family. Help me to remember to praise you always. Amen.

Think:

Why do you think the other nine lepers didn't return to Jesus to thank him?

Go Forth:

Make a gratitude list this week. Note down all the things you are grateful for and read through it during your prayer time, being sure to thank God for each one.

CHARITY
IS THAT WITH WHICH NO MAN IS LOST, AND WITHOUT WHICH NO MAN IS SAVED.

-St. Robert Bellarmine

TWENTY-NINTH SUNDAY IN ORDINARY TIME

A reading from the Book of Exodus
Ex 17:8-13

In those days, Amalek came and waged war against Israel.
Moses, therefore, said to Joshua,
"Pick out certain men,
and tomorrow go out and engage Amalek in battle.
I will be standing on top of the hill
with the staff of God in my hand."
So Joshua did as Moses told him:
he engaged Amalek in battle
after Moses had climbed to the top of the hill with Aaron and Hur.
As long as Moses kept his hands raised up,
Israel had the better of the fight,
but when he let his hands rest,
Amalek had the better of the fight.
Moses' hands, however, grew tired;
so they put a rock in place for him to sit on.
Meanwhile Aaron and Hur supported his hands,
one on one side and one on the other,
so that his hands remained steady till sunset.
And Joshua mowed down Amalek and his people
with the edge of the sword.

WHAT IMAGES CAME to mind as you listened to the reading? Draw or write about them here.

Responsorial Psalm

Ps 121:1-2, 3-4, 5-6, 7-8
R.(cf. 2) Our help is from the Lord, who made heaven and earth.
I lift up my eyes toward the mountains;
whence shall help come to me?
My help is from the LORD,
who made heaven and earth.
R. Our help is from the Lord, who made heaven and earth.
May he not suffer your foot to slip;
may he slumber not who guards you:
indeed he neither slumbers nor sleeps,
the guardian of Israel.
R. Our help is from the Lord, who made heaven and earth.
The LORD is your guardian; the LORD is your shade;
he is beside you at your right hand.
The sun shall not harm you by day,
nor the moon by night.
R. Our help is from the Lord, who made heaven and earth.
The LORD will guard you from all evil;
he will guard your life.
The LORD will guard your coming and your going,
both now and forever.
R. Our help is from the Lord, who made heaven and earth.

WHAT MAKES this psalm a hymn of praise?

A reading from the second Letter of St. Paul to Timothy

2 Tm 3:14-4:2

Beloved:
Remain faithful to what you have learned and believed,
because you know from whom you learned it,
and that from infancy you have known the sacred Scriptures,
which are capable of giving you wisdom for salvation
through faith in Christ Jesus.
All Scripture is inspired by God
and is useful for teaching, for refutation, for correction,
and for training in righteousness,
so that one who belongs to God may be competent,
equipped for every good work.

I charge you in the presence of God and of Christ Jesus,
who will judge the living and the dead,
and by his appearing and his kingly power:
proclaim the word;
be persistent whether it is convenient or inconvenient;
convince, reprimand, encourage through all patience and teaching.

WHY DOES St. Paul say Scripture is useful? Have you used Scripture in any of those ways? How?

A reading from the holy Gospel according to Luke

Lk 18:1-8

Jesus told his disciples a parable
about the necessity for them to pray always without becoming weary.
He said, "There was a judge in a certain town
who neither feared God nor respected any human being.
And a widow in that town used to come to him and say,
'Render a just decision for me against my adversary.'
For a long time the judge was unwilling, but eventually he thought,
'While it is true that I neither fear God nor respect any human being,
because this widow keeps bothering me
I shall deliver a just decision for her
lest she finally come and strike me.'"
The Lord said, "Pay attention to what the dishonest judge says.
Will not God then secure the rights of his chosen ones
who call out to him day and night?
Will he be slow to answer them?
I tell you, he will see to it that justice is done for them speedily.
But when the Son of Man comes, will he find faith on earth?"

WHAT EXAMPLES of faith have you seen in your daily life?

Pray:

Dear Lord, thank you for the gift of your word in Scripture. Thank you for providing me with guidance, with encouragement, with Truth. Let me hear your voice as I engage with Scripture. Help me to grow closer to you through it. Amen.

Think:

What value is there in reading Scripture? What makes it a worthwhile way to pass your time?

Go Forth:

Talk to your family about adding a nightly Scripture passage to your family prayer time. If you already do this with family, consider adding additional reading on your own.

DO NOT BE
AFRAID. DO NOT
BE SATISFIED
WITH
MEDIOCRITY.
PUT OUT
INTO THE
DEEP
AND LET YOUR
NETS DOWN FOR
A CATCH.
-St. John Paul the Great

21

THIRTIETH SUNDAY IN ORDINARY TIME

A reading from the Book of Sirach
Sir 35:12-14, 16-18

The LORD is a God of justice,
who knows no favorites.
Though not unduly partial toward the weak,
yet he hears the cry of the oppressed.
The Lord is not deaf to the wail of the orphan,
nor to the widow when she pours out her complaint.
The one who serves God willingly is heard;
his petition reaches the heavens.
The prayer of the lowly pierces the clouds;
it does not rest till it reaches its goal,
nor will it withdraw till the Most High responds,
judges justly and affirms the right,
and the Lord will not delay.

A FEW WEEKS AGO, we explored the meaning of the virtue of justice. How is that virtue displayed in today's first reading?

Responsorial Psalm

Ps 34:2-3, 17-18, 19, 23

R. (7a) The Lord hears the cry of the poor.
I will bless the LORD at all times;
his praise shall be ever in my mouth.
Let my soul glory in the LORD;
the lowly will hear me and be glad.
R. The Lord hears the cry of the poor.
The LORD confronts the evildoers,
to destroy remembrance of them from the earth.
When the just cry out, the Lord hears them,
and from all their distress he rescues them.
R. The Lord hears the cry of the poor.
The LORD is close to the brokenhearted;
and those who are crushed in spirit he saves.
The LORD redeems the lives of his servants;
no one incurs guilt who takes refuge in him.
R. The Lord hears the cry of the poor.

WHAT IMPACT DOES today's Psalm have on you? In other words, how does it encourage you or fortify you?

A reading from the second Letter of St. Paul to Timothy

2 Tm 4:6-8, 16-18

Beloved:
I am already being poured out like a libation,
and the time of my departure is at hand.
I have competed well; I have finished the race;
I have kept the faith.
From now on the crown of righteousness awaits me,
which the Lord, the just judge,
will award to me on that day, and not only to me,
but to all who have longed for his appearance.

At my first defense no one appeared on my behalf,
but everyone deserted me.
May it not be held against them!
But the Lord stood by me and gave me strength,
so that through me the proclamation might be completed
and all the Gentiles might hear it.
And I was rescued from the lion's mouth.
The Lord will rescue me from every evil threat
and will bring me safe to his heavenly kingdom.
To him be glory forever and ever. Amen.

WHAT VERSE OR verses stand out to you? What is God saying to you through them? Why?

A reading from the holy Gospel according to Luke

Lk 18:9-14

Jesus addressed this parable
to those who were convinced of their own righteousness
and despised everyone else.
"Two people went up to the temple area to pray;
one was a Pharisee and the other was a tax collector.
The Pharisee took up his position and spoke this prayer to himself,
'O God, I thank you that I am not like the rest of humanity --
greedy, dishonest, adulterous -- or even like this tax collector.
I fast twice a week, and I pay tithes on my whole income.'
But the tax collector stood off at a distance
and would not even raise his eyes to heaven
but beat his breast and prayed,
'O God, be merciful to me a sinner.'
I tell you, the latter went home justified, not the former;
for whoever exalts himself will be humbled,
and the one who humbles himself will be exalted."

How does today's Gospel further the discussion we've been having on the value of humility?

Pray:

Heavenly Father, I love you. I am grateful for all the blessings in my life. Help me to be like St. Paul, that I may run the race to its completion. You, Lord, are the center of my heart. Amen.

Think:

In today's Gospel, Jesus once again turns human perceptions and ideas upside down. What would people expect of the Pharisee (a religious leader) and the tax collector? What is Jesus revealing through this contrast?

Go Forth:

Make a plan for your week. What is one thing you can do each day to help you grow in your faith?

GOD DOES NOT REQUIRE GREAT ACHIEVEMENTS BUT A

HEART THAT HOLDS NOTHING BACK FOR SELF.

-St. Rose Philippine Duchesne

22

THIRTY-FIRST SUNDAY IN ORDINARY TIME

 reading from the Book of Wisdom
Wis 11:22-12:2

Before the LORD the whole universe is as a grain from a balance
or a drop of morning dew come down upon the earth.
But you have mercy on all, because you can do all things;
and you overlook people's sins that they may repent.
For you love all things that are
and loathe nothing that you have made;
for what you hated, you would not have fashioned.
And how could a thing remain, unless you willed it;
or be preserved, had it not been called forth by you?
But you spare all things, because they are yours,
O LORD and lover of souls,
for your imperishable spirit is in all things!
Therefore you rebuke offenders little by little,
warn them and remind them of the sins they are committing,
that they may abandon their wickedness and believe in you, O LORD!

How is God's mercy reflected in this passage from Wisdom?

Responsorial Psalm

Ps 145:1-2, 8-9, 10-11, 13, 14

R. (cf. 1) I will praise your name for ever, my king and my God.
I will extol you, O my God and King,
and I will bless your name forever and ever.
Every day will I bless you,
and I will praise your name forever and ever.
R. I will praise your name for ever, my king and my God.
The LORD is gracious and merciful,
slow to anger and of great kindness.
The LORD is good to all
and compassionate toward all his works.
R. I will praise your name for ever, my king and my God.
Let all your works give you thanks, O LORD,
and let your faithful ones bless you.
Let them discourse of the glory of your kingdom
and speak of your might.
R. I will praise your name for ever, my king and my God.
The LORD is faithful in all his words
and holy in all his works.
The LORD lifts up all who are falling
and raises up all who are bowed down.
R. I will praise your name for ever, my king and my God.

Why do we refer to God as the King, and to his people as the Kingdom?

A reading from the second Letter of St. Paul to the Thessalonians

2 Thes 1:11-2:2

Brothers and sisters:
We always pray for you,
that our God may make you worthy of his calling

and powerfully bring to fulfillment every good purpose
and every effort of faith,
that the name of our Lord Jesus may be glorified in you,
and you in him,
in accord with the grace of our God and Lord Jesus Christ.

We ask you, brothers and sisters,
with regard to the coming of our Lord Jesus Christ
and our assembling with him,
not to be shaken out of your minds suddenly, or to be alarmed
either by a "spirit," or by an oral statement,
or by a letter allegedly from us
to the effect that the day of the Lord is at hand.

TAKE a look at the second stanza. Based on what St. Paul is asking, what do you think has been happening to the community at Thessalonia? What sort of messages have they been receiving, and from whom?

A reading from the holy Gospel according to Luke

Lk 19:1-10

At that time, Jesus came to Jericho and intended to pass through the town.
Now a man there named Zacchaeus,
who was a chief tax collector and also a wealthy man,
was seeking to see who Jesus was;
but he could not see him because of the crowd,

for he was short in stature.

So he ran ahead and climbed a sycamore tree in order to see Jesus,

who was about to pass that way.

When he reached the place, Jesus looked up and said,

"Zacchaeus, come down quickly,

for today I must stay at your house."

And he came down quickly and received him with joy.

When they all saw this, they began to grumble, saying,

"He has gone to stay at the house of a sinner."

But Zacchaeus stood there and said to the Lord,

"Behold, half of my possessions, Lord, I shall give to the poor,

and if I have extorted anything from anyone

I shall repay it four times over."

And Jesus said to him,

"Today salvation has come to this house

because this man too is a descendant of Abraham.

For the Son of Man has come to seek

and to save what was lost."

WHAT IMAGES CAME to mind as you listened to the reading? Draw or write about them below.

Pray:

Lord, sometimes there are so many different voices vying for my attention that it is hard to focus on yours. Guide my ears, my eyes, and my heart, heavenly Father, so that my attention will be focused on you.

Think:

God is our King. What sets him apart from human kings throughout history?

Go Forth:

Take an example from Zaccheus this week. What belongings can you donate? Can you donate your time? What can you give to help those who need assistance? Make a list and serve those around you this week.

I AM A
SOLDIER OF CHRIST
-St. Martin of Tours

23

SOLEMNITY OF ALL SAINTS

 reading from the Book of Revelation
Rv 7:2-4, 9-14

I, John, saw another angel come up from the East,
holding the seal of the living God.
He cried out in a loud voice to the four angels
who were given power to damage the land and the sea,
"Do not damage the land or the sea or the trees
until we put the seal on the foreheads of the servants of our God."
I heard the number of those who had been marked with the seal,
one hundred and forty-four thousand marked
from every tribe of the children of Israel.

After this I had a vision of a great multitude,
which no one could count,
from every nation, race, people, and tongue.
They stood before the throne and before the Lamb,
wearing white robes and holding palm branches in their hands.
They cried out in a loud voice:

"Salvation comes from our God, who is seated on the throne,
and from the Lamb."

All the angels stood around the throne
and around the elders and the four living creatures.
They prostrated themselves before the throne,
worshiped God, and exclaimed:

"Amen. Blessing and glory, wisdom and thanksgiving,
honor, power, and might
be to our God forever and ever. Amen."
Then one of the elders spoke up and said to me,
"Who are these wearing white robes, and where did they come from?"
I said to him, "My lord, you are the one who knows."
He said to me,
"These are the ones who have survived the time of great distress;
they have washed their robes
and made them white in the Blood of the Lamb."

WHILE WE HAVE no firm idea of what heaven looks like, this passage from Revelation does give us a few ideas. If you were to base your description of heaven on the details given here, what would you say?

Responsorial Psalm

PS 24:1bc-2, 3-4ab, 5-6

R. (see 6) Lord, this is the people that longs to see your face.
The LORD's are the earth and its fullness;
the world and those who dwell in it.
For he founded it upon the seas

and established it upon the rivers.
R. Lord, this is the people that longs to see your face.
Who can ascend the mountain of the LORD?
or who may stand in his holy place?
One whose hands are sinless, whose heart is clean,
who desires not what is vain.
R. Lord, this is the people that longs to see your face.
He shall receive a blessing from the LORD,
a reward from God his savior.
Such is the race that seeks him,
that seeks the face of the God of Jacob.
R. Lord, this is the people that longs to see your face.

WHO ARE the people who long to see God's face? What makes this psalm a good choice for the feast of All Saints?

A reading from the first Letter of St. John

1 Jn 3:1-3

Beloved:
See what love the Father has bestowed on us
that we may be called the children of God.
Yet so we are.
The reason the world does not know us
is that it did not know him.
Beloved, we are God's children now;
what we shall be has not yet been revealed.

We do know that when it is revealed we shall be like him,
for we shall see him as he is.
Everyone who has this hope based on him makes himself pure,
as he is pure.

ACCORDING TO ST. JOHN, what blessings are bestowed upon the children of God?

A reading from the holy Gospel according to Matthew

Mt 5:1-12a

When Jesus saw the crowds, he went up the mountain,
and after he had sat down, his disciples came to him.
He began to teach them, saying:

"Blessed are the poor in spirit,
for theirs is the Kingdom of heaven.
Blessed are they who mourn,
for they will be comforted.
Blessed are the meek,
for they will inherit the land.
Blessed are they who hunger and thirst for righteousness,
for they will be satisfied.
Blessed are the merciful,
for they will be shown mercy.
Blessed are the clean of heart,
for they will see God.
Blessed are the peacemakers,

for they will be called children of God.
Blessed are they who are persecuted for the sake of righteousness,
for theirs is the Kingdom of heaven.
Blessed are you when they insult you and persecute you
and utter every kind of evil against you falsely because of me.
Rejoice and be glad,
for your reward will be great in heaven."

WHY DO you think the Sermon on the Mount was chosen for today's Gospel reading?
(Hint: read through the Beatitudes).

Pray:

Lord, make me a saint. Transform my heart and mold it to yours. Help me grow in
humility, faith, and love for you. Amen.

Think:

Read through the Beatitudes again. Think about which saints would match the spirit
of each beatitude and write that saint's name above.

Go Forth:

How can you make the beatitudes a reality in your life? In your home? In other words, what acts of faith or service can you do in order to live like a saint?

STRETCH EVERY FIBER OF MY BEING, DEAR LORD,

THAT I MAY FLY MORE EASILY TO YOU.

-St. Frances Xavier Cabrini

24

THIRTY-SECOND SUNDAY IN ORDINARY TIME

A reading from the second Book of Maccabees
2 Mc 7:1-2, 9-14

It happened that seven brothers with their mother were arrested
and tortured with whips and scourges by the king,
to force them to eat pork in violation of God's law.
One of the brothers, speaking for the others, said:
"What do you expect to achieve by questioning us?
We are ready to die rather than transgress the laws of our ancestors."

At the point of death he said:
"You accursed fiend, you are depriving us of this present life,
but the King of the world will raise us up to live again forever.
It is for his laws that we are dying."

After him the third suffered their cruel sport.
He put out his tongue at once when told to do so,
and bravely held out his hands, as he spoke these noble words:
"It was from Heaven that I received these;
for the sake of his laws I disdain them;
from him I hope to receive them again."
Even the king and his attendants marveled at the young man's courage,
because he regarded his sufferings as nothing.

After he had died,
they tortured and maltreated the fourth brother in the same way.
When he was near death, he said,
"It is my choice to die at the hands of men
with the hope God gives of being raised up by him;
but for you, there will be no resurrection to life."

WHICH VERSE OR verses from this reading stood out to you? Why?

Responsorial Psalm

Ps 17:1, 5-6, 8, 15

R. (15b) Lord, when your glory appears, my joy will be full.
Hear, O LORD, a just suit;
attend to my outcry;
hearken to my prayer from lips without deceit.
R. Lord, when your glory appears, my joy will be full.
My steps have been steadfast in your paths,
my feet have not faltered.
I call upon you, for you will answer me, O God;
incline your ear to me; hear my word.
R. Lord, when your glory appears, my joy will be full.
Keep me as the apple of your eye,
hide me in the shadow of your wings.
But I in justice shall behold your face;
on waking I shall be content in your presence.
R. Lord, when your glory appears, my joy will be full.

EXPLAIN TODAY'S PSALM RESPONSE. Why will our joy be full when the Lord's glory appears?

A reading from the second Letter of St. Paul to the Thessalonians

2 Thes 2:16-3:5

Brothers and sisters:
May our Lord Jesus Christ himself and God our Father,
who has loved us and given us everlasting encouragement
and good hope through his grace,
encourage your hearts and strengthen them in every good deed and word.

Finally, brothers and sisters, pray for us,
so that the word of the Lord may speed forward and be glorified,
as it did among you,
and that we may be delivered from perverse and wicked people,
for not all have faith.
But the Lord is faithful;
he will strengthen you and guard you from the evil one.
We are confident of you in the Lord that what we instruct you,
you are doing and will continue to do.
May the Lord direct your hearts to the love of God
and to the endurance of Christ.

WHY IS it important to pray for others and to ask others to pray for you?

A reading from the holy Gospel according to Luke

Lk 20:27-38 (OR Lk 20:27, 34-38)

Some Sadducees, those who deny that there is a resurrection,
came forward and put this question to Jesus, saying,
"Teacher, Moses wrote for us,
If someone's brother dies leaving a wife but no child,
his brother must take the wife
and raise up descendants for his brother.
Now there were seven brothers;
the first married a woman but died childless.
Then the second and the third married her,
and likewise all the seven died childless.
Finally the woman also died.
Now at the resurrection whose wife will that woman be?
For all seven had been married to her."
Jesus said to them,
"The children of this age marry and remarry;
but those who are deemed worthy to attain to the coming age
and to the resurrection of the dead
neither marry nor are given in marriage.
They can no longer die,
for they are like angels;
and they are the children of God
because they are the ones who will rise.
That the dead will rise
even Moses made known in the passage about the bush,
when he called out 'Lord, '
the God of Abraham, the God of Isaac, and the God of Jacob;

and he is not God of the dead, but of the living,
for to him all are alive."

THE SADDUCEES ATTEMPT TO trick Jesus with a trick question. How does Jesus' answer prove he knew what they were trying to do?

Pray:

Heavenly Father, the world is heading into a busy season. Soon it will be Advent, and the world around us will be focused on material gifts. Keep my focus on you, Lord, as we begin to approach another holy season of waiting. Thank you, Lord. Amen.

Think:

Look back at the way Jesus treats the Sadducees in today's Gospel. What surprises you about his treatment? Why is it surprising?

Go Forth:

Make a list of people you would like to pray for. They can be people you know personally or people you've never met. Devote some of your prayer time this week to lifting up their intentions, whether you know their intentions specifically or not.

THE DEVIL IS
ALWAYS
DISCOVERING
SOMETHING
NOVEL AGAINST
THE

TRUTH.

-St. Leo the Great

25

THIRTY-THIRD SUNDAY IN ORDINARY TIME

 reading from the Book of Malachi
Mal 3:19-20a

Lo, the day is coming, blazing like an oven,
when all the proud and all evildoers will be stubble,
and the day that is coming will set them on fire,
leaving them neither root nor branch,
says the LORD of hosts.
But for you who fear my name, there will arise
the sun of justice with its healing rays.

LIST A FEW WAYS TO keep your house in order. In other words, how can you and your family prepare for Jesus' return on a daily basis?

Responsorial Psalm

Ps 98:5-6, 7-8, 9

R. (cf. 9) The Lord comes to rule the earth with justice.
Sing praise to the LORD with the harp,
with the harp and melodious song.
With trumpets and the sound of the horn
sing joyfully before the King, the LORD.
R. The Lord comes to rule the earth with justice.
Let the sea and what fills it resound,
the world and those who dwell in it;
let the rivers clap their hands,
the mountains shout with them for joy.
R. The Lord comes to rule the earth with justice.
Before the LORD, for he comes,
for he comes to rule the earth,
he will rule the world with justice
and the peoples with equity.
R. The Lord comes to rule the earth with justice.

WHAT DOES the justice of the Lord look like? For an extra challenge: what does the justice of the Lord look like in the Old Testament? In the New Testament? What similarities and differences do you see?

A reading from the second Letter of St. Paul to the Thessalonians

2 Thes 3:7-12

Brothers and sisters:
You know how one must imitate us.
For we did not act in a disorderly way among you,
nor did we eat food received free from anyone.
On the contrary, in toil and drudgery, night and day
we worked, so as not to burden any of you.
Not that we do not have the right.
Rather, we wanted to present ourselves as a model for you,
so that you might imitate us.
In fact, when we were with you,
we instructed you that if anyone was unwilling to work,
neither should that one eat.
We hear that some are conducting themselves among you in a disorderly way,
by not keeping busy but minding the business of others.
Such people we instruct and urge in the Lord Jesus Christ to work quietly
and to eat their own food.

WHAT IS St. Paul encouraging the Thessalonians to do? How might following St. Paul's directions help them grow in virtue?

A reading from the holy Gospel according to Luke

Lk 21:5-19

While some people were speaking about
how the temple was adorned with costly stones and votive offerings,
Jesus said, "All that you see here--
the days will come when there will not be left
a stone upon another stone that will not be thrown down."

Then they asked him,
"Teacher, when will this happen?
And what sign will there be when all these things are about to happen?"
He answered,
"See that you not be deceived,
for many will come in my name, saying,
'I am he,' and 'The time has come.'
Do not follow them!
When you hear of wars and insurrections,
do not be terrified; for such things must happen first,
but it will not immediately be the end."
Then he said to them,
"Nation will rise against nation, and kingdom against kingdom.
There will be powerful earthquakes, famines, and plagues
from place to place;
and awesome sights and mighty signs will come from the sky.

"Before all this happens, however,
they will seize and persecute you,
they will hand you over to the synagogues and to prisons,
and they will have you led before kings and governors
because of my name.
It will lead to your giving testimony.
Remember, you are not to prepare your defense beforehand,
for I myself shall give you a wisdom in speaking
that all your adversaries will be powerless to resist or refute.
You will even be handed over by parents, brothers, relatives, and friends,
and they will put some of you to death.
You will be hated by all because of my name,
but not a hair on your head will be destroyed.
By your perseverance you will secure your lives."

WHAT IS God's promise to his people in today's Gospel?

Pray:

Heavenly Father, it is not easy to be a Catholic today. It is not easy to live our Catholic faith when so many forces and ideas want to push against it. But we know that the battle has already been won, and we know that you will always guide and protect us. Help me to rest in the knowledge that you are my Father and you will watch over me all the days of my life. Amen.

Think:

Which reading stood out the most to you? Why? Tell your parents which scripture you chose and explain why it spoke to you.

Go Forth:

How well can you defend your faith? Take some time this week to learn about any Church teaching of your choosing. Ask your parents or pastor for ideas.

THE MEASURE OF
LOVE IS TO LOVE
WITHOUT
MEASURE.
-St. Francis de Sales

26

THE SOLEMNITY OF OUR LORD JESUS CHRIST, KING OF THE UNIVERSE

 reading from the second Book of Samuel
2 Sm 5:1-3

In those days, all the tribes of Israel came to David in Hebron and said:
"Here we are, your bone and your flesh.
In days past, when Saul was our king,
it was you who led the Israelites out and brought them back.
And the LORD said to you,
'You shall shepherd my people Israel
and shall be commander of Israel.'"
When all the elders of Israel came to David in Hebron,
King David made an agreement with them there before the LORD,
and they anointed him king of Israel.

JESUS IS a direct descendant of King David. In what ways are King David and Jesus Christ's kingships different from one another?

Responsorial Psalm

Ps 122:1-2, 3-4, 4-5

R. (cf. 1) Let us go rejoicing to the house of the Lord.
I rejoiced because they said to me,
"We will go up to the house of the LORD."
And now we have set foot
within your gates, O Jerusalem.
R. Let us go rejoicing to the house of the Lord.
Jerusalem, built as a city
with compact unity.
To it the tribes go up,
the tribes of the LORD.
R. Let us go rejoicing to the house of the Lord.
According to the decree for Israel,
to give thanks to the name of the LORD.
In it are set up judgment seats,
seats for the house of David.
R. Let us go rejoicing to the house of the Lord.

WHO WERE the twelve tribes of Israel? Ask your parents' permission if you need to research the answer.

A reading from the Letter of St. Paul to the Colossians

Col 1:12-20

Brothers and sisters:
Let us give thanks to the Father,
who has made you fit to share
in the inheritance of the holy ones in light.
He delivered us from the power of darkness
and transferred us to the kingdom of his beloved Son,
in whom we have redemption, the forgiveness of sins.

He is the image of the invisible God,
the firstborn of all creation.
For in him were created all things in heaven and on earth,
the visible and the invisible,
whether thrones or dominions or principalities or powers;
all things were created through him and for him.
He is before all things,
and in him all things hold together.
He is the head of the body, the church.
He is the beginning, the firstborn from the dead,
that in all things he himself might be preeminent.
For in him all the fullness was pleased to dwell,
and through him to reconcile all things for him,
making peace by the blood of his cross
through him, whether those on earth or those in heaven.

ACCORDING TO ST. PAUL, who is Jesus? Use quotations from the scripture to support your answer.

A reading from the holy Gospel according to Luke

Lk 23:35-43

The rulers sneered at Jesus and said,
"He saved others, let him save himself
if he is the chosen one, the Christ of God."
Even the soldiers jeered at him.
As they approached to offer him wine they called out,
"If you are King of the Jews, save yourself."
Above him there was an inscription that read,
"This is the King of the Jews."

Now one of the criminals hanging there reviled Jesus, saying,
"Are you not the Christ?
Save yourself and us."
The other, however, rebuking him, said in reply,
"Have you no fear of God,
for you are subject to the same condemnation?
And indeed, we have been condemned justly,
for the sentence we received corresponds to our crimes,
but this man has done nothing criminal."
Then he said,
"Jesus, remember me when you come into your kingdom."
He replied to him,
"Amen, I say to you,
today you will be with me in Paradise."

Aside from Jesus, who do you find most admirable in this passage? Why?

Pray:

Lord, you are the King of my heart. I love you with all my mind and all my spirit. Keep me grounded in your love and focused on your will for my life. Amen.

Think:

In which of today's readings is God portrayed as a merciful king? Use specific examples form the scripture to help support your answer.

Go Forth:

Make an Advent plan with your family. How will you celebrate Advent in your home in preparation for the coming of Christ Jesus?

EVEN ON THE
CROSS HE DID NOT
HIDE HIMSELF
FROM SIGHT;
RATHER, HE MADE
ALL CREATION
WITNESS TO THE
PRESENCE OF ITS
MAKER.
-St. Athanasius

27

SAINT FEAST DAYS

June

1. St. Justin
2. Sts. Marcellinus and Peter
3. St. Charles Lwanga and Companions
5. St. Boniface
6. Mary, Mother of the Church
9. St. Ephrem
19. St. Romuald
21. St. Aloysius Gonzaga
22. St. Paulinus of Nola; Sts. John Fisher and Thomas More
23. Nativity of St. John the Baptist
24. Sacred Heart of Jesus
25. Immaculate Heart of Mary
28. St. Iraneus
29. Sts. Peter and Paul
30. The First Martyrs of the Holy Roman Church

July

1. St. Junipero Serra
3. St. Thomas the Apostle
5. St. Antony Zaccaria, St. Elizabeth of Portugal
6. St. Maria Goretti
9. St. Augustine Zhao Rong and Companions
13. St. Henry
14. St. Kateri Tekawitha
15. St. Bonaventure
16. Our Lady of Mt. Carmel
20. St. Apollinaris
21. St. Lawrence of Brindisi
22. St. Mary Magdalene
23. St. Bridget
24. St. Sharbel Makhluf
26. Sts. Joachim and Anne
29. Sts. Martha, Mary, and Lazarus
30. St. Peter Chrysologus
31. St. Ignatius of Loyola

August

2. St. Eusebius of Vercelli; St. Peter Julian Eymard
4. St. John Vianney
7. St. Sixtus II and Companions; St. Cajetan
9. St Teresa Benedicta of the Cross
10. St. Lawrence
11. St. Clare
12. St. Jane Frances de Chantal
13. Sts. Pontian and Hippolytus
14. St. Maximilian Kolbe
19. St. John Eudes
20. St. Bernard
21. St. Pius X
24. St. Rose of Lima
25. St. Bartholomew
25. St. Louis; St. Joseph Calasanz

27. St. Monica
28. St. Augustine
29. Passion of St. John the Baptist

September

3. St. Gregory the Great
8. The Nativity of the Blessed Virgin Mary
9. St. Peter Claver
13. St. John Chrysosotom
14. Exaltation of the Holy Cross
15. Our Lady of Sorrows
16. Sts. Cornelius and Cyprian
17. St. Robert Bellarmine and St. Hildegard of Bingen
20. Sts. Andrew Kim Tae-Gon and Paul Chong Ha-Sang
21. St. Matthew
23. St. Pius of Pietrelcina
27. St. Vincent de Paul
28. St. Wenceslaus; St. Lawrence Ruiz and Companions
29. Sts. Michael, Gabriel, and Raphael
30. St. Jerome

October

1. St. Therese of the Child Jesus
2. The Holy Guardian Angels
4. St. Francis of Assisi
5. Blessed Francis Xavier
6. St. Bruno; Blessed Marie Rose Durocher
7. Our Lady of the Rosary
9. St. Denis and Companions; St. John Leonardi
11. St. John XXIII
14. St. Callistus I
15. St. Teresa of Jesus
16. St. Hedwig
18. St. Luke
19. Sts. John de Brebeuf and Isaac Jogues
20. St. Paul of the Cross

22. St. John Paul the Great
23. St. John of Capistrano
24. St. Anthony Mary Claret
28. Sts. Simon and Jude

November

1. All Saints' Day
2. All Souls' Day
3. St. Martin de Porres
4. St. Charles Borromeo
10. St. Leo the Great
11. St. Martin of Tours
12. St. Josaphat
13. St. Frances Xavier Cabrini
15. St. Albert the Great
16. St. Margaret of Scotland; St. Gertrude
17. St. Elizabeth of Hungary
18. St. Rose Philippine Duchesne
22. St. Cecelia
23. St. Clement I; St. Columban; Bl Miguel Agustin Pro
24. St. Andrew Dung-Lac and companions
25. St. Catherine of Alexandria
30. St. Andrew, Apostle

ABOUT THE AUTHOR

Ginny Kochis is an author, blogger, and homeschooling mom of three from Northern Virginia who believes God gives curious, creative, intense children the exact mother they need to thrive. Through her website and online community, Ginny provides practical support and prayerful encouragement to Catholic moms raising the differently wired.

Find more resources and join 3500 moms in the Not So Formulaic community at www.notsoformulaic.com.

ALSO BY GINNY KOCHIS

To Hear His Voice: A Mass Journal for Catholic Kids (Years A, B, and C)

Made for Greatness: A Growth Mindset Journal for Courageous Catholic Youth

God's Kintsugi: A Catholic Devotional for Moms of Differently-Wired Kids

Made in United States
Orlando, FL
04 May 2022

17514505R00104